Probing the Unknown

Other Books by MAURICE WOODRUFF

Know Tomorrow Today
Woody
The Secrets of Foretelling Your Own Future
You and Your World

Probing the Unknown

The Personal Experiences of a Psychic

Maurice Woodruff

Cowles Book Company, Inc.
New York

COPYRIGHT © 1971 BY MAURICE WOODRUFF

SBN 402-12631-9

LIBRARY OF CONGRESS CATALOG CARD NUMBER 79-118897

COWLES BOOK COMPANY, INC.
A SUBSIDIARY OF COWLES COMMUNICATIONS, INC.

PUBLISHED SIMULTANEOUSLY IN CANADA BY
GENERAL PUBLISHING COMPANY, LTD.
30 LESMILL ROAD, DON MILLS, TORONTO, ONTARIO

PRINTED IN THE UNITED STATES OF AMERICA

FIRST EDITION

To my friend
Mavis Gough
With appreciation for her help
and encouragement on this book

Contents

1. What It Feels Like to Be Maurice Woodruff   1
2. Prophetic Devices   17
    Phrenology   18
    Cartomancy   21
    Telepathy   34
    Palmistry   36
    Astrology   38
    Astrology and Mating (Sex)   75
    Dice   81
    Personal Features   83
3. Dream Interpretations   90
4. Responsibilities of Being a Psychic   123
5. Reminiscences   139
6. Reincarnation (Immortality)   161
    My Spiritual Experiences   168
7. Clairvoyance/Astrology and Religion   180
8. Personal Questions   184
    Index   193

Probing the Unknown

1.
What It Feels Like to Be Maurice Woodruff

Quite often people say to me, "What does it feel like to be Maurice Woodruff the clairvoyant?" Well, I would like to make it very clear that it feels no different from having been born Bill Smith or Tom Grant. It is my honest and sincere belief that every single one of us is psychic—maybe not continuously, but at some point in life. How many times have *you* said, "I knew very well that was going to happen," when you didn't really know it at all? Women call this knowledge intuition; men call it a hunch. Some men like to go even further and flatter themselves that it is business acumen. In some cases it is, but in more cases than not it is a psychic flair of which they are unaware.

It also has been said that women are more psychic than men. Of course, I do not agree, although I have always thought women to be the stronger of the two sexes, not,

Probing the Unknown

as we are led to believe, the weaker. My only explanation for the origin of this idea is that men are basically the providers of the home and family while women are the defenders of these institutions. More often than not, the woman is clever enough to put an idea into her husband's head and then eventually persuade him that he thought of it first.

I have met many women and men in my life, both through my private readings and my public appearances, and I have learned that as well as being a clairvoyant/astrologer I have to be somewhat of a psychologist. When a person has a private sitting with me, I always say to him, "I am going to tell you the bad as well as the good."

A good nine out of ten always respond, "Oh, yes! That's what I want"—but of course I make sure this is the case.

I never inform anyone that he is going to die, because I think this would be very wrong indeed and would worry him, although I may inform one of his relatives in order to help the relative when the event takes place.

As an example, there is a very rich businessman in England whose name is Jerry Rex. He and I have become close friends over the years, even though our first meeting was as client to clairvoyant. There is hardly a film, television show, or play put on throughout the world for which Jerry does not make the hairpieces, beards, sideburns, and the like. Some years ago Jerry came to me for a reading, and unfortunately I had to tell Jerry that his father-in-law would soon die. I explained at the time that the only reason I was telling him this was because Jerry's wife, Helen, was an only child and I knew that her father's death would hit her rather badly.

I said to Jerry, "By your knowing this now, it will cushion the blow for Helen later."

What It Feels Like to Be Maurice Woodruff

He said, "Well, you are pretty right about most things, Maurice, but in this case I think you could be wrong, because my father-in-law, Louis, had a thrombosis some four or five years ago, but the doctors have now declared him to be a very fit man."

A short time later, I was down for a weekend at my country house in England. Jerry telephoned me to ask, "Maurice, you know that Louis and Sadie [his father- and mother-in-law] have never seen your country house and it's such a lovely day, do you think we could drive down?"

I naturally said that I would be delighted for them to come. As it turned out, it was a beautiful hot day. We had tea in the gardens and we took pictures of Louis and Sadie, truly wonderful people; they hadn't been photographed together for many years.

Everything was extremely happy, but as Jerry, Helen, and Helen's parents left that evening to drive home, I turned to my manager, Harry Arnold, and without their hearing I said, "That's the last you are going to see of Louis."

"Oh, don't say such things as that," he responded.

Unfortunately, the following Friday Louis died, and Jerry telephoned me and said, "Thank God you forewarned me that this might happen, Maurice, because I would never have known how to deal with Helen. As it is, now I have her taking it very calmly."

A few years ago, when I was in Beverly Hills, Peter Sellers telephoned and asked me to come to see him at his cottage on the grounds of the Beverly Hills Hotel. During the reading I said to Peter, "Now, you take extra care, Peter, because, while nothing too bad is going to happen, I am not awfully happy about that which I am seeing."

Probing the Unknown

Peter appeared to take this quite well, and I went back to my apartment in Westwood. A short while afterward Bert Mortimer, Peter's valet-companion and chauffeur, telephoned and said, "Maurice, Pete's a little worried about what you said regarding your unhappiness about what you have seen. Is this going to be anything very tragic?"

I replied, "No, Peter is going to be a sick man, but just as long as he behaves well, he will be okay."

It is now past history about Peter having that heart attack at Cedars of Lebanon Hospital.

I point out these cases to you as an example that I do tell the bad as well as the good. It is a well-established fact that nothing happens to you in life, except death, that is so bad that a compensation does not eventually follow; thus the sitter wants so much to get toward the good that he will automatically accept the bad. Any reputable and reliable clairvoyant will do this. I do *not* foretell death at any time unless for the reasons I have mentioned above, and since I am only human, I of course could be wrong. I know of no clairvoyant/astrologer who can with all honesty claim 100 percent correct predictions.

A certain titled lady in England came to see me for a private reading some time ago. Unknown to me, she had apparently met me before at a charity affair, where I had said that she might have some concern about her young son but that she should not worry because she would have another boy.

When this lady sat down in front of me I could see that her hands were perspiring through nervousness, and I said to her, "You had a son, and it is very necessary to have a son, an heir to carry on your husband's title. You lost that son while you were abroad. I am now going to tell you that you will have another son. He will be born at seven months and I am also going to tell you that it

What It Feels Like to Be Maurice Woodruff

will be a most difficult birth but the child will be a boy and will be very healthy."

The lady looked at me and said, "Is that all you have to tell me?"

I replied that it was, whereupon she proceeded to tell me that she had met me first in the late Queen Mary's old home, Marlborough House, where I was working for a charity fete. When one does work for these parties, the idea is to get as many people in and out as quickly as possible in order to make the most money for the charity. The lady had come to me at that fete for a reading and I had told her that she had a son, would lose that son while she was away, but should not worry because she would have another child that would be a boy. She had thought this was really all rubbish. A week later her husband had taken her to the Brussels fair in Belgium and while they were on the trip their little son had caught a nasty cold, developed pneumonia, and died.

The lady said, "Mr. Woodruff, that having come true shattered me somewhat and I apologize for having ridiculed your prediction after I last saw you, and I am now back to you again. As you must know, my husband is one of the wealthiest men in England. We have been to the leading gynecologists all over the world, because I am at the moment in very early pregnancy. They have said that either I have the child removed or I shall lose my life and that of the child. We are exceptionally happy, yet at the same time must have an heir to carry on the title. I have told my husband that I will not give my answer to these gynecologists without having seen you first. What have you got to say?"

I replied, "As I told you before, you are going to have an exceptionally bad time, but you will have a boy child born to you, very healthy, at seven months." She went away much calmer and happier than when she first arrived to see me.

About four months later (and this has rarely happened to me), I had a night when I was not sleeping too well and, for no reason whatsoever, I suddenly thought of this woman and wondered how right, or how wrong, I would be, because, after all, I then realized what a terrific responsibility I had placed upon my own shoulders. I am delighted to be able to tell you that I have the christening card of the boy who was born at exactly seven months and is now quite healthy.

I make predictions quite spontaneously, without thought. If one sits for a test for extrasensory perception at a psychic research center one can't pause and think before answering. I have found that what I say in a spontaneous fashion has a far greater degree of accuracy than what I might give quite a lot of thought to. I had such an experience when I made predictions for the English performer, Danny La Rue.

I first met Danny La Rue in London in 1963 where I was introduced to him by my good friend, Harry H. Corbett. Danny was then appearing nightly at Winstons Night Club in Mayfair, and I made some predictions about him:

First, he would open his own nightclub within a year.

Secondly, he would appear in a big theater in the West End of London in his own show.

Danny looked aghast and, although he did not condemn what I had said as being of no value, I knew that he thought I was a little crazy. Shortly thereafter I went to Hollywood where I was scheduled to fulfill some contracts and see some clients.

I returned to London in April, 1964, and expected to

What It Feels Like to Be Maurice Woodruff

go immediately to my own house. Instead, I was met at Heathrow Airport by someone who whisked me away in a car to Tenterden Street, Hanover Square. I was not told the final destination, but when I saw Danny La Rue as I entered the club I realized it was his establishment. After his show, Danny came over to my table and said, "How right you were, Maurice—now what have you got to tell me?"

I then predicted that he would have his own show in a small theater in London's West End and that he would have one success after another. My friendship with Danny has extended over many years, and I can honestly say that he deserves this marvelous success because he is such a nice person. Never have I heard him make a derogatory remark about anyone.

It is past history now, but Danny did open in London's Whitehall Theatre in his own show that was called *Come Spy With Me*, and appeared in the royal gala shows as well as at his own club in Hanover Square. He has also drawn big audiences with his act at the Palace Theatre in London.

During the run of my television series, "Maurice Woodruff Predicts," I recall one program when I had the beautiful actress Gena Rowlands as a guest. Miss Rowlands is married to one of my favorite actors, John Cassavetes. On the program, I predicted in front of my audience of a few million people that Gena would have a baby girl and I said that the child would be born just before John completed his next movie. In June, 1970, Gena gave birth to a baby girl while John Cassavetes was editing the final touches of his film, *Husbands*, with Peter Falk and Ben Gazzara.

Peter Sellers clearly thought I was talking through my hat in 1957. Face to face with him in my consulting room,

Probing the Unknown

I could see the skepticism in his eyes as I predicted his future. "Your radio work has made you a household name in Britain," I said. "But now you are about to start an entirely new career, which will earn you a worldwide reputation."

Peter cocked a quizzical eyebrow.

I told him, "Before long you'll be offered a contract for your first film. You'll play the part of a lay-about, a wide boy, a small-time crook. Then a man with a z in his name will approach you; he will ask you to play more than one character in a film that will really put you on the map."

Peter kept a straight face—but I was not surprised to hear later that he had only come to me as a joke. When I switched on my radio in England to the "Goon Show," a zany comedy program, that week I half expected to hear the Goons make clairvoyance the brunt of their jokes.

It was a serious Peter who telephoned me several months later to ask for an appointment. He was about to start filming *The Lady Killers*, with the now Sir Alec Guinness. And he was playing a small-time crook. He had also been offered a contract by director Mario Zampi to film *Your Past Is Showing*, in which he was to play five different characters.

I predicted that it would be a wise move for him to accept the part of the shop steward in the film *I'm All Right, Jack*. He was a little concerned that people would think it out of character for an actor who had made his name in crazy comedy, but he took my advice—and won the Film Academy Award for the best performance by a British actor in 1959.

I predicted that he would have a daughter and forecast her birth date. I also told him that his first record, "The Best of Sellers," would be a hit in England. He did not believe me, but it sold over 100,000 copies.

What It Feels Like to Be Maurice Woodruff

Since then, as you possibly know—if you saw Peter on my television show in America—he has been both a client and a very good friend.

I remembered very well that first meeting with him when I read a newspaper interview a few years ago in which Peter said: "I never make up my mind about any important matter without a visit to Maurice Woodruff. And nine times out of ten he's right."

I have never claimed to be a miracle worker. No clairvoyant can honestly claim to be 100 percent accurate in every prediction he makes. I calculate that I have been right 75 percent of the time, which others say is not a bad average.

The strange thing is that I cannot look into my own future. I have known only one clairvoyant who could do so—my late mother, Vera Woodruff.

One evening in April, 1957, as my mother lay seriously ill in a London hospital, my sister-in-law went to see her. They were chatting quietly about this and that when my mother suddenly looked at her and said, "It will happen at two thirty on the twenty-third." My sister-in-law immediately assumed my mother was talking about an operation and upon leaving the hospital she asked a doctor just how serious it would be.

The doctor looked puzzled. "There was no question," he said, "of operating. Mrs. Woodruff is suffering from hypertension."

My mother died at 2:30 P.M. on April 23 of that year, exactly as she had forecast.

She was a truly remarkable character. Born in a small country village in Suffolk, England, she came to London at the age of seventeen to take a job as maidservant to a titled society lady. Within twenty years she was recognized in Britain as the greatest clairvoyant of her time. The

Probing the Unknown

Duchess of Windsor, in the days when she was still Mrs. Simpson, consulted my mother, who predicted her marriage to the then King, now the Duke of Windsor. I remember seeing the charming note the Duchess wrote shortly before the abdication shocked the country.

My mother's uncanny psychic powers led stars and statesmen alike to seek her advice. I count myself lucky indeed to have inherited her gift.

In the twenty-three years since I began to practice clairvoyance seriously, I have come to know, as intimately as only a psychic can, many of the most interesting people of our time. While I was in Tangier, Morocco, in 1959, Barbara Hutton invited me to her fabulous home in what was once the sultan's palace. Behind the high wall that hides the palace from the bustling Casbah, candlelight gleamed on rich tapestry studded with pearls and rubies as Arab servants served exotic dishes prepared by a chef who had been brought over from Paris. Amid such signs of wealth, Barbara herself was dressed with striking simplicity in an ice-blue gown, her only jewelry a single-strand pearl necklace.

I liked her. I found her a charming woman who possessed a delightful sense of humor. After dinner, Barbara and I left the others and went to the superb throne room where low couches, scattered with jewel-encrusted cushions, surrounded a tree in the center of the room and growing up through the ceiling. The eyes are the mirrors of the soul, and as I looked into Barbara's eyes I told her, "Your son will have an accident in a fast car." Her son, Lance Reventlow, did have an accident, although I did not know at the time that he had become a racing driver.

"You are not happy now about his future, but when

What It Feels Like to Be Maurice Woodruff

you meet his wife, you and she will get on well together. As for your future, I predict that before 1963 you will marry again."

She looked away for a moment, twisting the magnificent ring on her left hand. "No," she said, "I shall never marry again. I've finished with men."

As we all know, Barbara did marry again within a year.

Barbara asked me, as so many people do, "What's your secret? Is it telepathy? Thought-reading? Some form of spiritualism?"

I told her, "It is not telepathy. How could it be when I can describe to most people things they have long forgotten and foretell events happening in the future of which they know nothing? It is not thought-reading. I regard that as pure hokum. It is not spiritualism. I claim no link with departed spirits, although I genuinely think that I am guided in some way and I am absolutely convinced that spiritualism exists."

When a client comes to see me, I simply look into his eyes. They are the only part of a person that can never be disguised.

As I study eyes, pictures, words, and feelings come crowding into my mind, and I am able to probe the past and predict the future.

Two very definite things I make a strong point of not foretelling unless absolutely necessary. First, as I have already noted, I will not tell the person himself that he will die, because I feel this will be of no help whatsoever to him. I know of only one occasion when I did intimate to a person that he was going to die, and this was during the World War II years.

The wife of a stockbroker named Alfred Chenhalls used to come to see me for consultation. I could see that she had been behaving very badly toward her husband, and I also could see that he had another lady around him who was showing him a lot of attention.

I told his wife that she should be much nicer to him. Basically she was a fine person and at one time had been first violinist in the Indian Philharmonic Orchestra. If she was not agreeable to her husband, I felt that she would be the loser of a considerable amount of money.

Next, I saw Chenhalls himself and pointed out his wife's good qualities. I then advised him to change his will, or make a new one, because I did not think that he would be happy about the one he had either made or was about to make. Knowing that he had a journey to take, I also asked him to please change his flight reservation. As it transpired, Alfred Chenhalls, who so closely resembled the late Sir Winston Churchill, was on a plane bound for Lisbon. His plane crashed, and on board at the same time was the famous film star Leslie Howard. Luckily, Chenhalls had made a new will just one week prior to taking this journey and had canceled out his old will, in which he left his money to the other woman. He was a considerably wealthy man, and of course his wife then became a rich widow.

The second thing I will not advise about, either on television, on stage, or with private clients, is the stock market, or gambling. I make a very strong point of this, simply because I feel that if a person spent only a small amount of money, such as four or five dollars, and lost it, then I would be responsible, and, as I have said, I am not infallible.

There are also situations in which I will not do a reading. I can be turned off by the attitude of a client, and in this case the client becomes the loser. An example of this

What It Feels Like to Be Maurice Woodruff

occurred a few years ago when a new prospect was brought along to see me by an old client.

As she came into my consulting room and sat down, I looked at her and said, "This may sound quite crazy, but I see a whip around your head." She looked at me rather facetiously and laughed, and I thought I was obviously off on the wrong track. Then I said, "You have got a son," and again came this rather rude laughter. I became annoyed and told her that there was nothing more I could or would tell her. I suggested to her that she find some other clairvoyant, for by this time all my Arian fire was up.

"But you *must* tell me," she pleaded. "What will my friend think if I leave so quickly?"

"It's none of her business," I said. "And, having known her so long, I am certain that she will not even ask. Remember that my work is confidential, and I do not discuss one client with another!"

The lady kept me arguing back and forth for some period of time and then left, and my old client finally came in and had a reading.

Several days later the old client telephoned me and said, "Maurice, you've let me down for the first time ever, and I have sent you so many people who have all come away with glowing reports about you. My friend tells me that you told her a lot of rubbish."

"For your information," I replied, "I only had a chance of saying two things to her. First, I said she may think it sounded stupid, but I saw a whip around her head and, second, I said she had a son."

My old client was amazed and said, "Well, of course you would get a whip around her head. She is Mrs. Mills, the wife of the biggest circus owner in England, com-

Probing the Unknown

parable to the American Ringling Brothers. She came to see you especially about her son, so you were right, Maurice, and she was stupid to be so facetious, because you might have been able to help her."

You can imagine the many parties and cocktail parties to which I get invited throughout the year. I get turned off when a person comes up to me at one of these affairs and either demands predictions or says, "Well, of course, I don't really believe in your work. Nobody's ever been able to tell me anything, and I do not suppose that you could either!" I know when a person wants a reading or a prediction and does not have the honesty to ask for it outright or acknowledge belief in my work. On the other hand, a person can demand it of me as though I were at the party for that special reason. After all, invariably I am a guest, the same as he is.

I well remember a very big party in New York in 1969 where I saw a lady who was absolutely decked out in diamonds and obviously was extremely wealthy. She came across the room and said to me, "So what have you got to say to me?" I replied that I had nothing to say to her. She then said, "But isn't that what you are here for? To make predictions?" I thought this rude, but was not about to spoil the party. Once again, my Arian impudence came to the fore. "No, I am here as a guest, the same as yourself, and in any case, with all the diamonds that you are wearing tonight, if I did make a prediction for you, I would have to make it wholesale!" I admit that this was rude of me, but her approach to me was hardly that of a diplomat, and I am trying to point out to you just what will turn me off. If a person asks me for a reading in a nice manner, or if I think that a person needs me to make a

What It Feels Like to Be Maurice Woodruff

prediction for him, then I am the very first one to do this, without any hesitation.

I have often been asked whether people do possess the power to curse. There is little doubt that certain people do. As you have been told, my mother was a foremost clairvoyant of her day, and one learns from the experience of others. My mother had a difficult life inasmuch as she had a husband who was of very little help to her. She had to support him and their seven children. In those days life was more of a struggle than it is today because there were no benefits to be had. Quite naturally there were moments when she lived upon her nerves, and, being a Taurian, she possessed the Taurian characteristics of the bull, which when maddened will flay at the matador. Twice throughout her life I remember her making a curse against someone, and twice those curses came about. They so horrified me that I swore I would never curse anybody, even if I was enraged.

The first occasion was when my mother was working at a very big society party given by the late Sir Sefton Branker. Lady Branker, his wife, had been an invalid for some years and had to use a wheelchair. My mother was extremely fond of her, as she was of Sir Sefton himself. At this particular party, Sir Sefton had asked my mother whether he would marry another lady who was present, and my mother had answered quite outspokenly, because she was an extremely honest person, that he would not, because the present Lady Branker would live for many years.

At the dinner party later that night, Sir Sefton, who had possibly had one drink too many, stood up and made a rather detrimental remark about my mother.

Probing the Unknown

This annoyed her very much and, like the Taurian bull, she stood up and said, "For saying that, you will come down in the flames of hell within the next month." You may remember that Sir Sefton Branker was the captain of the zeppelin *R101*. Within a month of the dinner party, the zeppelin did burst into flames in midair over London and came down with everyone aboard losing his life.

The second time concerned a gentleman friend of my mother's who was treating his wife very badly. This gentleman's wife was going through her menopause and the doctors had warned the husband that any undue upsets could unbalance her mind. My mother arrived at their home one Sunday morning when the man was haranguing his wife. In a rather Victorian, dramatic manner, my mother got herself between them and told him that he should behave himself better. He in turn was exceptionally rude to my mother.

Finally she said to him, "For saying those things to me, and treating your wife so badly, your tongue will be cut out within a year." The outcome of this was that the wife did, in fact, lose her sanity and was put into an asylum. Nine months later the husband developed cancer of the tongue, and his tongue had to be removed. In fact, this was the first such operation performed in the Middlesex Hospital in London.

# 2.

Prophetic Devices

There are many methods of foretelling the future—some in which I have great faith and belief, others that I seek to avoid, but I would like to make it very clear that there are several mediums a person may choose from in selecting one to foretell your future. If the person is not a charlatan (and there are many), the medium he selects will allow him the best level of concentration. I use a person's eyes; some people use playing cards, others a crystal ball. There is the established science of palmistry —reading the lines on the palms. Other prophetic devices are phrenology and, of course, the oldest one in history— astrology.

Although I use a person's eyes when giving a clairvoyant reading, I am also an astrologer. I use no other devices apart from these two methods. Here are a few of these various ways of foretelling the future.

Probing the Unknown

Phrenology

Phrenology, a psychic science, claims the existence of a correlation between the shape of the skull and certain human traits. A Viennese physician, Franz Joseph Gall, pioneered studies in this field. His extensive research, begun in 1796, led him to assign each of man's distinctive traits of character or mental function to a corresponding section of the brain, which was supposed to develop locally in conjunction with that particular function. He did stress, however, that a strongly developed propensity would not always be attended by a protuberance of the brain and a corresponding bump on the skull.

Gall also concluded that the skull molds itself over the brain during infancy and, after full development of the head has been attained, the skull's simulated brain surface produces bumps that may be analyzed by a phrenologist. When Gall's followers later misused and perverted his findings by making spurious claims, people forgot his outstanding contributions to cerebral physiology.

I believe that humans and animals possess intellectual minds in varying degrees. As I write this chapter, my thoughts about phrenology involve a mental action and I am able to grasp my pen through a mechanical action of the muscles that obey a mandate of the mind that becomes a cerebral action.

Phrenologists divide the head into three main sections:
1. The lower portions of the back of the head are known as the region of instincts or propensities.
2. The upper portion of the head is occupied by the sentiments or moral faculties.
3. The front of the head, including the forehead, contains the abilities or intellectual faculties.

Prophetic Devices

Over the years, subdivisions have been made in these three mains sections, and through the impressions or depressions of the noted areas one can determine how a person will behave in a given circumstance. For example, you can sometimes observe that the section of the forehead just above the eye protrudes more in some people than in others. This indicates whether or not a person has a well-balanced sense of proportion.

A profile of a head is helpful in the explanation of its various sections and the reading of the bumps. If you draw a line from the center of the head at the top to a point in front of the ear, this section halfway between the top of the head and top of the ear will tell us whether a person is aggressive or reticent. This is indicated by a slight bump that can be found in this area on most people through a fingertip examination. If the bump is pronounced, it suggests that this person would like things done in an efficient and impressive manner. If the bump is not all that noticeable, then it points out that the person is satisfied with himself and will have a more retiring nature.

A pronounced bump in the area located above the nape of the neck and indented slightly toward the ear indicates that a person is very affectionate and above average in his sexual desires. You can often find another bump placed on top of the previously mentioned spot, which points to the fact that the person is extremely friendly. You will thus know that this person enjoys other people's company and does not like to be left too much on his own.

If you proceed to a section of the profile just above and to the right of the ear and find a bump there, it suggests that the person is methodical and capable of good concentration. If the person possesses a bump immediately above the ear, at the side of the head, then you may be

Probing the Unknown

assured that he has terrific energy and has the potential to become a top executive in business.

Again, as you consult the profile of the person where you have drawn your line, take the section vertically halfway down from the top of the head to the side of the face and search for a bump. If you discover one, there is a good possibility that the person is extremely kind and sympathetic and can be depended on to give sensible assistance and guidance. A bump located in the next area, toward the front of the head, informs you that this person is also very generous and charitable by nature.

If you check the area of the profile immediately above the eyebrow, you should be able to find three slight bumps, although these will be more pronounced in some people than in others. The bump nearest to the bridge of the nose suggests that the individual will be adept at judging values and may have a keen sense of distance and of weights and measures. The second bump, situated halfway across the eyebrow, shows the extent of a person's color sense. If it is pronounced, then the person will rarely be wrong concerning his judgment of color. The bump that you can sometimes feel toward the end of the eyebrow nearest the ear is what I have named the methodical one; if it is pronounced, you can be reasonably certain that the person works out an almost faultless method for doing any particular task.

If you find a pronounced bump in the center of the area just behind the ear, the characteristics suggested are a love of life and the instinct to resist illness by possessing just that little extra energy that pulls one through a time of trouble.

A bump that can be felt on the forehead toward the hairline at the left side of the face points out that the person is very genial and can be quite passive in his approach to life.

The section of the profile halfway between the top of the ear and the eyebrow may contain a bump that will indicate the person has a tendency to acquire and collect unusual possessions.

I have given you information that, from my experience, has proved to be correct in many cases. If you make a point of trying to study the science of phrenology, then you may use the guide I have outlined as a basis to judge the character of your subject. Of course, you can integrate these characteristics in order to ascertain how a person will react in a particular situation.

Cartomancy

Cartomancy merely portrays the reading of the past, present, and future by means of a deck of playing cards and is fairly widely used by mediums throughout the world. The interesting point about cartomancy is that apparently each medium who "reads the cards" seems to give his own meanings to each individual card. I am one of the many people who believe that the reading of cards can be highly accurate if done by a reputable person. When I was much younger, I used to give my readings by this method, until in 1957 I was asked to appear in London's Café de Paris, where it was thought to be too chic for me to be using cards upon a table. It was at this point that I started to give my readings by looking at the person's eyes.

The late Donald Campbell, a very dear friend, asked me one day how to read the cards. Donald was a great believer as well as an ardent spiritualist—spiritualism being another means or device to foretell events, one in which I completely believe, although I have always advised against its use. If you have lost someone very dear to you, let him rest. If he wants to come back and give you a message, my belief is that he will do so of his own volition. This can also become an obsession.

Donald Campbell set speed records on land and sea in cars and boats with the name *Bluebird* designated for each one. It was evident to me that he had a death wish, and he had many narrow escapes from disaster during his racing career.

I had explained to him the meaning of certain cards when they appeared in combination with other cards. The night before Donald attempted to break the existing speed record in his racing boat, he proceeded to cut his own cards. I had firmly advised against his cutting his own cards because it is supposed to be most unlucky.

Donald cut up the ten of spades, the queen of spades, and the ace of spades upside down. This, indeed, was most unfortunate.

The next day he raced his boat on a lake in England and broke the speed record from one shore to another. On the return leg of the trip he was overheard on the radio to utter these words, which were his last: "My God, she's going, I can't hold her, I'm lost."

Donald Campbell's body was never found.

Donald had tremendous sympathy and patience for others and it is my opinion that he would have made a wonderful medium. I well remember one particular story Donald told me that gives evidence of his psychic power. Donald broke the land speed record in Australia in his car, the *Bluebird*. The car had to have special tires because at the end of each trip the tires would be almost

Prophetic Devices

in ribbons. Donald had made the first trip and was sitting in his car while the mechanics and fitters quickly got it ready for his return trip. He told me that he felt positively ghastly, when he suddenly looked up above the dashboard and to his surprise saw his late father, Sir Donald, standing there. His father said to Donald in a very clear voice, "Don't worry, son, you are going to make it."

Donald told me that all fear then left him, and he made the return trip with all the confidence in the world and broke the land speed record at that time.

Cards have been used to foretell the future throughout the centuries. Some say that this method originated in ancient Egypt; others believe that it dates back even further in history to the early Hindus who brought cartomancy to Egypt when some of them migrated west.

I have absolute faith in the prognostications of the cards, but I am firmly convinced that it is not wise for amateurs to use this method on total strangers; like so many other ways of foretelling the future, it could be highly depressive or dangerous.

Here is a list as a guide to the meaning of all the fifty-two cards in a pack.

Playing Cards

HEARTS (The luckiest suit in the whole pack)

ACE	There will be talk of either a change of residence or of your making some alteration in where you live.
TWO	You will be receiving a telephone call or cable of some importance.
THREE	Not important.

Probing the Unknown

FOUR	There will be talk of your crossing a body of water, or you can expect a visitor from across the water.
FIVE	You could look for good news within five days or five weeks. Also at times this can represent the initial E, for someone who is very fond of you.
SIX	Of little importance.
SEVEN	You will have dealings with someone whose initials are GJ.
EIGHT	Someone of the opposite sex will try to have a flirtation with you—eight can also mean the initial H.
NINE	This is generally known as the "wish" card; it denotes that you are going to be very lucky and all should turn out well for you.
TEN	This indicates security and foretells that you will surmount most of your difficulties.
JACK	Happy news is on its way to you. This will cause excited chattering.
QUEEN	A lady with gray eyes can be an exceptionally good friend to you, provided that you do not cross her.
KING	A man, over the age of thirty-five, with bluish gray eyes, although difficult, will help you over an obstacle.

CLUBS

ACE	Events will be improving for you from lunchtime onward, especially toward evening, and you would do well to leave your important moves until after lunch.
TWO	Your irritations and frustrations will leave you within a matter of two months.

Prophetic Devices

THREE	Not important.
FOUR	You will be offered a change of some kind to which you would do well to give strong thought before arriving at a decision.
FIVE	You can expect to take a short trip out of town in the near future.
SIX	Someone with the initial F or P is trying to get in touch with you.
SEVEN	A surprise gift is on its way to you.
EIGHT	Not important.
NINE	Take care that you do not let the world know your business; otherwise you will be extremely angry with someone close to you.
TEN	This usually concerns your business affairs and the club suit indicates that you must give more attention to them.
JACK	A young brown-eyed man who is genuine, yet intense, will surprise you by his good advice.
QUEEN	Take care, for you have a sharp-tongued gossiper around you.
KING	A man with brown or hazel eyes who is thirty years old or over may be difficult, but do not fight him.

DIAMONDS

ACE	Your financial affairs should take a turn for the better within the next month.
TWO	You will be having dealings with someone whose initial is B.
THREE	Something on which you have been concentrating should develop within three days or three weeks.

Probing the Unknown

FOUR — Either you or someone closely connected to you will be offered a change in business that should prove to be an excellent opportunity.

FIVE — This indicates uncertainty for you and you could be faced with some indecision.

SIX — Not important.

SEVEN — Not important.

EIGHT — You are being deceived by someone near you; do not believe everything that you are told.

NINE — After a short period you will come out of your difficulties and most things should be advantageous for you and there is happiness ahead.

TEN — Your business affairs should take a turn for the better, giving you more peace of mind.

JACK — This indicates that there is pleasant chattering going on about you. It can also have the unfortunate meaning of adultery.

QUEEN — A lady with blue eyes is a good friend of yours, but can be rather vicious to those she dislikes.

KING — Either you or a relative will be paying a visit to the doctor in the near future.

SPADES

ACE — Right side up: You should watch your health, or someone around you is sick. Upside down: You will hear of a death.

TWO — You will reach an agreement by letter or sign a contract in the near future.

THREE — You may find yourself having to complete a task very quickly, so that most of what is going on around you will have to be done in a rush.

Prophetic Devices

FOUR	Try not to make any changes in your life for the moment; it would be better for you to maintain your usual patterns of existence.
FIVE	You are worrying about something going on around you. Try to remember that as long as you worry, you cannot think clearly.
SIX	Not important.
SEVEN	You will hear of a parting between two people.
EIGHT	You will find yourself having to deal very shrewdly with someone whose initial is H.
NINE	You will be faced with some difficult situations, but as long as you make the other people initiate the actions, you will come out of this all right.
TEN	You are going to be dealing with a very tough business person and therefore will have to stick rigidly to your point in order to attain your goals.
JACK	A black- or green-eyed man who takes himself rather seriously has very genuine liking for you.
QUEEN	Take care what you tell to a black- or green-eyed woman who is either a widow or a divorcée.
KING	You will be paying a visit to the dentist in the very near future.

When a reading of the cards is given, it is difficult to obtain real accuracy. Some folk, you will find, use only twenty-six playing cards from an ordinary pack, but I use the whole deck. I shall try to explain one of the many ways in which I would give a reading:

First, you ask your sitter to shuffle the pack, and at the same time make a wish, and then give the pack back to you.

Then, as though dealing, you lay seven cards face

Probing the Unknown

downward upon the table, separately, with a space between each one. Dealing straight from the pack, you repeat this step five times, placing one card upon another, so that you are left with seven lots of five cards separate from each other, lying face down on the table.

You pick up one lot at a time and give your reading from each one separately. In this particular reading, my client is a brown-eyed, middle-aged gentleman. On the opposite page is an illustration of a sample reading.

You must pick up each separate pack of five cards and lay them down fanwise, face up upon the table, so that your first fan will read, from left to right:

5 of SPADES	indicates worry
10 of SPADES	indicates business affairs
QUEEN of SPADES	a lady with green or black eyes
KING of CLUBS	a man with brown or hazel eyes, over thirty
3 of SPADES	something done very quickly

This, in turn, tells me that a green- or black-eyed lady, who thinks very highly of the brown-eyed middle-aged gentleman, is worried about his business affairs. But there will be a quick answer regarding this. The three of spades signifies a rush.

The next lot of five cards laid down face upward on the table in the illustration:

9 of HEARTS	the wish card
QUEEN of HEARTS	a lady with blue or gray eyes

Prophetic Devices

Herewith the layout of the seven lots of five cards.

29

Probing the Unknown

5 of DIAMONDS	indicates slight uncertainty or indecision
9 of DIAMONDS	in this instance the second-best wish card
8 of DIAMONDS	unimportant here

This second lot causes me to feel much happier, because I know that the brown-eyed gentleman is going to be given great help by a blue- or gray-eyed lady after some indecision. The fact that the nine of hearts, which is the wish card, and the nine of diamonds, the second wish card, are in that pack of five pleases me, because they indicate happiness.

Now let us take a look at the third lot of five cards:

9 of SPADES	my sitter's depression
10 of CLUBS	represents business, financial security, or government
QUEEN of DIAMONDS	in this instance, good news
7 of HEARTS	person whose initials are G or J
4 of CLUBS	represents a change being offered

I know that after some uncertainty and anxiety the gentleman will receive the offer of a change in his business by someone whose initial could be G or J.

Now let us take a look at the fourth lot of five cards. Here I am more pleased, because I see:

KING of HEARTS	a man above the age of thirty with blue or gray eyes
JACK of HEARTS	happy news

Prophetic Devices

KING of DIAMONDS   a doctor
7 of CLUBS   unimportant here
QUEEN of CLUBS   brown- or hazel-eyed lady

The jack of hearts is a sign that happy news is coming to our sitter. We know he has not been feeling terribly well of late, by the king of diamonds, because that is usually a doctor. The sitter will be told something to his advantage by a lady who gossips slightly, and has brown or hazel eyes.

We now turn our fifth lot of five cards face up on the table, and here we see, from left to right:

7 of SPADES   indicates a parting
9 of CLUBS   the change could anger our client
2 of HEARTS   speed card
4 of DIAMONDS   a happy change card
3 of HEARTS   overrules the anger of the 9 of clubs

This suggests that someone associated with our sitter has been threatening to leave him quickly, because the two of hearts denotes a telephone call, a cable, or a communication that arrives very quickly. The change that the four of diamonds indicates is for the sitter's good because it is followed by a heart, namely the three of hearts.

We now pick up the sixth lot of five cards, and place these face up on the table, and here we find, from left to right:

10 of DIAMONDS   good business affairs
8 of CLUBS   in this instance the initial H
6 of HEARTS   not too important

Probing the Unknown

5 of CLUBS	indicates a trip after midday
ACE of CLUBS	the evening or nighttime card

From the ten of diamonds we gather that the gentleman will be getting greater peace of mind from his business. Normally, the eight of clubs is not of great importance, but in this instance, similar to the G or J that we mentioned in an earlier lot, it will be helpful to him. There could also be the initial H associated with this help, because the eighth letter of the alphabet is *h*. This is followed by the six of hearts, which indicates happiness but has little significance here. The five of clubs tells us that he will have to take a trip, either in the afternoon or evening, for an interview regarding his business.

We now pick up the last lot of five cards, and place these face upward on the table. These read, from left to right:

ACE of HEARTS	residence
JACK of DIAMONDS	exciting or happy news
KING of SPADES	this invariably connotes the dentist
6 of SPADES	not important
6 of DIAMONDS	again, usually not important

From this we gather that his worries are unfounded, because happy news is coming to his house. He may have to visit the dentist, but the fact that he has two sixes side by side only strengthens the pleasing surprise that is coming his way.

We now count the number of hearts in the seven lots, and they come to nine. Since the average number is

Prophetic Devices

Seven lots of five cards with the tens separate and the double wish card separate.

33

usually seven or eight, when giving a person a reading in which he has made a wish, we are not unhappy. Had the sitter cut up all thirteen hearts we would have been delighted. We then look to see if he has got his wish among his seven lots. We notice that he has it, as well as the nine of diamonds, which in this case would act as a double wish card.

We then look to see how many tens he has picked out, and we find that he has the ten of spades, the ten of clubs, and the ten of diamonds (three out of four). Basically we glean from this reading that, even though he has been very worried about his business affairs, he has also wished upon them, and he will get his wish sooner than he had thought.

I would term this a very happy reading for the sitter.

There are endless combinations you can obtain by dealing out a pack of cards, but I do not have the space here to work these all out for you. I would suggest you try to work these out for yourself by using the basic principles that I have given you. Bear in mind that it takes careful thought, and is not easy. Try cartomancy on close relatives, not strangers, and have fun.

Telepathy

Telepathy is the transference of thought by a means other than the five senses.

Someone asked me recently whether I had heard from a very distant relative of mine of whom I am not overly fond, and my reply was, "No, and for the Lord's sake do not mention him, otherwise I shall hear."

Oddly enough, by the very next post I received a letter from this distant relative. It was quite obvious to me that this mention of him by my friend had trans-

Prophetic Devices

ferred itself to this relative's mind, which, in effect, is telepathy.

How often have you heard of one twin sensing, or knowing, that the other twin was unwell, or in slight trouble, when they were many miles apart. It is possible because the link between them is extremely strong. This can happen to anyone with whom you are closely connected, for I have proved to myself that if you sit quietly and concentrate, you are able to pass a message over to a person who is many miles distant from you.

I well remember a story the late Simone Silva, a beautiful actress, told me in 1956. One night during World War II she awoke from a deep sleep and could not stop thinking of a relative whom she had not seen in many years. She felt certain that this relative, who lived in Egypt, was in some way in danger from a knife. As it transpired, several weeks later she heard by mail that her cousin had cut himself badly while trying to open a tin of food; unfortunately, the cut had become infected and he had to have his hand amputated.

The late Jack Hilton, who was one of England's top theatrical impresarios and a famous bandleader, once told me about a quarrel he had with a lady friend. She told him later that she had made a wish that he would fall when conducting his orchestra. He had no knowledge of this at the time, but he found for two or three nights in succession that he had to hold on to the rostrum for fear of falling. His legs seemed to have no strength in them, yet as soon as he came off the platform, he felt fit and well and full of energy. Quite naturally, he went to see his doctor, but the doctor could find nothing wrong with him. I would call this telepathic willing of evil.

Where telepathy is concerned, three conditions must exist: First, one or other of the two people involved must possess a certain amount of extrasensory perception (ESP); second, there must have been, or still could be, a very great closeness with the person to whom you are sending out your telepathic message, or vice versa; third, on these occasions either of you must be so strong-minded that you are able to free your mind completely of other things and concentrate in order to send that message over long distances.

Basically, I know from my own personal experience that this device definitely exists, but would not recommend it to be used unless you are sure of your strength of will. Furthermore, you must always remember that this is to be used for the good, and not the ill, of another person.

My own mother awoke one night during World War I and saw a vision of a very dear male friend who was away fighting in Flanders. She had a dream that he was crossing a bridge; she could hear gunfire; in her high state of emotion she screamed out to him to go back and walk under the bridge.

When he returned some two years later, he informed us that he had been crossing a bridge, amid heavy firing, and he had the strangest compulsion to turn back and walk under the bridge. He did so, and even though the firing under the bridge was equally heavy he got across safely, while most of the boys who had gone over that bridge were shot or maimed.

Unexplainably strange, but nevertheless true.

Palmistry

Yet another method of ascertaining the future is palmistry, and it is only within the last few years that this has been officially recognized as an actual science. There are

Prophetic Devices

still some people who do not believe it is possible to foretell events by this method. Yet I have found that I have been pleasantly surprised when the skeptic has, on many occasions, admitted to me that he has now become a believer.

I well remember when Ann Warner, the wife of Jack Warner of Warner Brothers fame, gave a dinner party in Hollywood. One of her guests was involved in production, concentrating on drama and comedies. When I took a look at his hand I predicted, "Before the year is over, you will be making musical films again."

He laughed uproariously and replied, "Boy, are you way out! I will not make a musical and neither will Warner Brothers. There is no question about this."

Yet before the year had passed Warner Brothers was making *The Music Man*, which we all know was followed by *My Fair Lady*, and if these are not musicals, then palmistry is not palmistry.

On another occasion, I was introduced to a very beautiful blonde young lady during my first visit to Hollywood in 1960. Without asking any questions, I looked at her palm and told her that she was an actress but she had not yet made her mark. I also said, "You will be offered a part in a film in which your face and clothes will be very dirty, and you will not have to say one single word. Your first impression will be to refuse this part because you have nothing to say. Please be guided by me and accept it, because it will not only get you great publicity, but it will also make you a star." The beautiful girl was Stella Stevens, and she was offered a role in the television series, "Bonanza," in which she had to play the part of a deaf mute. As a result of this she received very high praise indeed, and she has since gone on to become a big star. You have not yet seen the best of

Probing the Unknown

Stella Stevens, for she will, in my opinion, become one of the really great stars of the seventies.

A familiar sight at most fairgrounds or on the pier of seaside resorts is the lady palmist who can usually be found sitting in her booth. Regardless of what skeptics may say, the palmist nearly always has quite a long queue of people waiting to have their palms read. You can see, from the following diagram, the different lines that tell the palmist how to read a future. The desire to know one's future, regardless of the devices or means employed to obtain this information, is booming throughout the entire world as never before.

Astrology

Astrology, of course, can be a very great help in many areas. It has been studied over the years by the keenest minds and appeals very much to the intellectual side of one's nature. It takes into consideration a person's life from the moment of his birth; the length of time between conception and birth is also a factor, as well as the type of birth—natural or cesarean. This will have a definite influence on his development and will help to determine his limitations as well as his assets. It aids in adaptation to one's environment and in guiding one's energies in order to gather the most fruitful harvest. It clearly explains our antipathies and our sympathies, and shows us why we dislike some people, yet are magnetically drawn toward others. It produces a better understanding of other people and their actions by giving us a clear insight into their characteristics.

Astrology brings into creative use our perception and judgment, teaching us when to be impartial and to use

Prophetic Devices

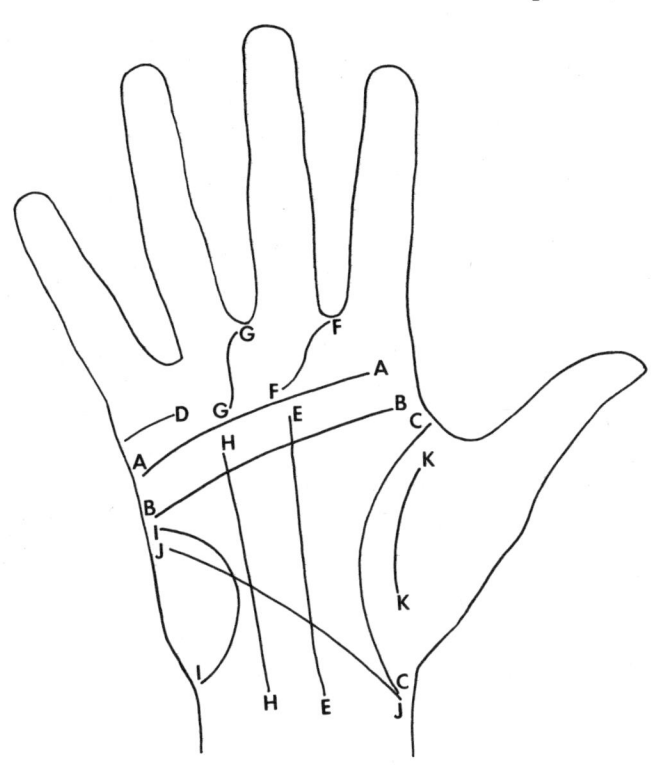

A	Heart line	G	Intuition line
B	Head line	H	Line of success
C	Life line	I	Another line of intuition
D	Marriage line	J	Line of health
E	Fate line	K	Line of influence
F	Girdle of Venus		

discrimination in reaching a careful conclusion. Its universal study has undoubtedly influenced world thought and attitudes, especially in the past ten years. Because of this, we have almost attained a universal intelligence permeating all beings, thus helping us to greater understanding.

Misfortunes can be prevented through astrology by guiding a person away from calamities, enabling him to act wisely and discreetly. No one has thus far been able to succeed in proving this method to be false. If you ask many men and women what their birth signs are, nine out of ten will tell you without hesitation. They will usually be able to inform you, too, of the designations proved by experience throughout the centuries to bring luck to the sign of the zodiac; these include days, months, colors, and jewels.

There are two great principles of the positive and the negative: the sun is positive, the center of force, gives out energy, and therefore is constructive and creative; the moon is negative, in effect a reflector of light, and therefore a preserver, a molder, which is a formative condition. The three most important factors in astrology are known as the sun, the moon, and earth, which, in other words, are spirit, soul, and body. The sun, the force of energy, represents the individual and guides his mental and moral expression. The moon, the soul, deals with all the personal characteristics and the way we express ourselves, whether emotional or otherwise, and determines our outgoing attitudes—in other words, our personality. The earth is represented by the sign of the zodiac at the time of birth and typifies the behavior and expression of its subject; it allows the ego to have free expression through personality.

Prophetic Devices

The Planets

Seven of the planets, in addition to the earth, sun, and moon, are influences on the zodiac. Pluto has no significant influence on the zodiac and is not usually taken into consideration. Here are the other planets in the order of their nearness to the sun:

Mercury, as the name implies, is mercurial, changeable, and dry. This planet forms the rational and intellectual faculties, and those who are born under its influence are very susceptible to atmospheric pressures and conditions peculiar to surroundings.

Venus, which I believe is the most beautiful planet in the solar system, brings with it the influence of good fortune, harmony, and temperate behavior. Almost all of its influence is directed toward affection, happiness, and pleasure.

Mars, by nature a hot planet, would naturally have an influence almost the opposite from that of Venus. Mars governs with force and can often be quite unfeeling and harsh; it is more independent of the other planets and has a very definite influence on the sun, rather than being controlled by it. One could say that Venus represents the feminine sex and Mars represents the masculine sex.

Jupiter has been known universally as the planet of blessing and good fortune, because most of its vibrations are harmonious, and its conditions are justice and peace, combined with sympathy and compassion. Those people who come under its influence are invariably sincere, warmhearted, joyously hopeful, and truthful.

Saturn by nature is a restricting, limiting, and binding planet. Although, in effect, it is the extreme opposite of Jupiter, in many respects it pairs off with that planet,

Probing the Unknown

but generally Saturn is considered to be a malefic influence of bad fortune.

Uranus brings the highest of intelligence in its path. Its vibrations can be thought of as the octave, as it were, of the planet Mercury, and it influences those people who think ahead of their time and are certainly not conventionalists by nature. People who are born under the influence of this planet are indeed fortunate because they have almost etheric brains; they have their own ideas, free from personal bias or public opinion. It has been said that this planet acts upon the nerves and magnetic conditions and relates in some ways to the utility and purpose of certain portions of man's anatomy that have baffled medical science.

Neptune may or may not have any influence. It is open to serious question. It is accepted that the telepathic sense and the intuitive faculty are invariably prominent in people born under this planet, and genius has frequently stemmed from Neptune. This is always dependent on the planet to which Neptune is conjoined at birth. It would appear that Neptune augments and specializes in the faculties, so that in such cases it would not be surprising that, conjoined with genius, there would be concomitant traces of insanity. It is also a fact that the borderline between genius and insanity is often imperceptibly fine.

In the following pages I am going to give you the individual characteristics pertaining to those who are born in each month of the year. These will of course be generalized. In their main features they will predominate over all the planetary aspects, though in any given case they are apt to be largely modified by the rising sign and the positions and aspects of the planets. The characteristics are proved accurate. Even where exceptions are encountered, however, it will usually be found that the quality is definitely present in the person, but may be transmuted so as to be barely recognizable.

ARIES (March 21 to April 20). Aries is the first and the strongest sign of the zodiac. Its subjects are very true to the symbol of their sign, a ram possessing rather formidable horns. The ram uses his horns to gain supremacy over an adversary and the Arian, too, by nature makes his point in an aggressive manner.

Those born under this sign are rulers and pioneers; they always want to be at the head of whatever they set out to do. Arians are only satisfied when things are going their way; they do, in consequence, quite often fail as employees. They are dogmatic to the point of self-righteousness, but in the long run are usually proved right.

Because of their foresightedness about what lies ahead for them, they are able to plan for what is most likely to happen. Arians are better as supervisors than having to take orders and directions from others; they are capable of leading in a strangely accomplished manner, but at times they cannot be relied on to do a job competently themselves. The expression jack-of-all-trades applies very well to Arians.

They love to travel and usually do a great deal of it. They like change, want to be on the move, and never seem to want to stay put in any one situation or place.

All told, Arians are very headstrong, enthusiastic, and impulsive. They can be self-willed to the point of annoyance when they feel that they are on to a good thing. It is best to avoid crossing them, for if you do, you will see all discretion thrown to the wind and feel the lash of their tongues.

If you make a friend of an Arian, you would find it

Probing the Unknown

hard to find a more genuine person, for they can be extremely gentle as well as outspokenly frank. One of their well-known faults is to be almost stupidly overgenerous—to the point of embarrassment.

Arians born between March 21 and March 31 ordinarily possess quick tempers, which can become quite uncontrollable at times. They are known to act on impulse but their willpower drives them stubbornly to complete their plans with consistent success. They form strong opinions that they defend with dogged determination.

April 1 to April 10 subjects are among the cleverest members of this sign. They give the impression of weakness but they give way only when this can lead to an eventual attainment of their goals. They are usually gifted with vivid imaginations, which have proved to be one of their strongest assets. Experience has shown them to be the most affectionate and faithful people of this sign.

April 11 to April 20 subjects most closely resemble the symbol of Aries, the ram. They seem to rush headlong into situations with little or no outward demonstration of fear. They have a profound sense of loyalty and protection toward friends and loved ones. This group varies from one extreme of temperament to another. They might wish to give someone the world one day and want to murder him the next.

Arians can have two distinct traits: They can possess a rather cocksure and overconfident nature that, while being strongly sensitive, is more inclined to be jealous and dogmatic. They can also be very ambitious and appreciative of everything that is done to help them; they often show a great desire to help weaker people.

Constitutionally, Arians are fortunate because their

Prophetic Devices

health is usually very good. However, they can be affected by headaches and sinus conditions, and by strain and overwork. On the whole, they live long lives, but nearly always find they have to wear glasses later on in life.

"Luck-bringers" for Arians:

The best colors for them are all shades of red, especially scarlet or bright red.

Their jewel, which they nearly always wear, is the diamond.

The most propitious days of the week for them are likely to be Tuesdays or Thursdays.

The month: Good fortune is distributed throughout the year, particularly in the autumn months, so I cannot single out any one month for Arians.

As a point of interest—Arians should try not to associate with Scorpions in business or even socially.

Their best marriage partners are selected from the Leo group (July 22 to August 21) or from Gemini (May 21 to June 20).

Should the choice be a Leo subject, then a very agreeable and very self-controlled partner may be expected. The Arian will have to be very tactful at times, because an angered Leo subject may be apt to take action without warning, letting emotions overrule caution, and it is often difficult to know what has caused the anger. However, Leos can be extremely sympathetic.

On the other hand, should the choice be a Gemini subject, the Arian will find an intellectual mate who does not allow emotions to rule him. Gemini and Arian subjects are similar in that they do not like to be in one place too long; they thrive on change. Never try to force a Gemini to finish one thing before starting another. If

45

Probing the Unknown

you wish him to do something your way, explain very clearly what you think should be done—and in this way avoid rebellion against you.

TAURUS (April 21 to May 20). Taurus is the second sign of the zodiac. It is a very fixed sign and most Taurians are practical and solid types. At times they can be most reserved and also most determinedly stubborn.

Their greatest assets are patience, reliability, and honesty, and with these qualities they make very capable executives. You should know what you are up against before trying to fool Taurian subjects because they have very quick, sharp minds and tongues.

Taurians keep their emotions and their energies well controlled, but beware if they are provoked; if they are driven too far they see red, and could well resemble the symbol of their sign, the bull.

Taurians are often greatly influenced by outstanding experiences, and from the thoughts and feelings that come from this they can well be described as psychic types. When they concentrate in this field, they can be quite accurate.

The mate who tries to deceive a Taurian partner is at a disadvantage; quite often Taurians will surprise even themselves by relating something about either the past or the future seemingly out of the blue, with no previous knowledge, and this will turn out to be true. I feel that their great intuition comes about because they are naturally fatalists, which helps them to control their emotions.

Financially a Taurian either makes a great deal of money or nothing worthy of mention. He is also marked by contrasts in his personality—one may be lazy or stubborn while another is unselfish, generous, and at times overenergetic.

Prophetic Devices

Taurians born between April 21 and April 30 most likely have a stubborn nature; they do not change their minds without a great deal of persuasion. They enjoy feeling needed by others but they can also indulge themselves in periods of laziness.

May 1 to May 10 subjects could excel in positions as buyers because they are gifted with excellent powers of discrimination. There are times when they are needlessly thrifty, causing others to think of them as being penurious, but they would no doubt be sincerely shocked if anyone informed them of this. Their astute business minds tend to overrule their personal relations with friends, and this can occasionally cause unintentional hurt. They are ambitious, but not greedy, and their sense of practicality helps them to ascertain when it is wise to pass by an opportunity.

May 11 to May 20 subjects are apt to be generous but this can sometimes be dogmatic, especially when they think it will be helpful to close associates. They will do anything within reason for others without thought of compensation. This genuine unselfishness is often exploited by their foes, and they must be always aware of that fact. They have a will of iron and members of this group do not usually become failures. They place heavy demands on those who work for them and insist on perfection, often when it is not entirely necessary.

Taurians are successful in most things. They do well in trades or professions that demand high standards of practical ability plus strong determination. Although they are not particularly quick in financial matters, it would be difficult to fool them in this field.

Constitutionally, Taurians are lucky; they usually have good health because they don't overdo things. They preserve their good health, which alleviates most health problems for them. Heart conditions could trouble them later in life. The throat and kidneys are their weakest points.

"Luck-bringers" for Taurians:

The colors best for them are all shades of blue.

Their jewel is the emerald, although I have learned that the ruby is lucky for them, too.

The day of the week for important developments is either Monday or Friday.

The month that brings good results for them is October.

Ideal marriage partners for them are from Virgo (August 22 to September 21) or Capricorn (December 21 to January 19).

They can expect a Virgo partner to be very methodical and at times quite critical. Virgoans do not like to waste time on dreaming, are very intelligent and "cool"; they will always have one eye open for opportunities. It is much better to leave this type alone if they show the desire to argue; by doing this, chances are they will come around to your side much quicker.

If a Taurian chooses a Capricornian for his partner, he will find someone who is very ambitious for his or her spouse and ever ready to help his or her advancement to some high position. Capricornians can be irritating at times because of their overcautiousness; they also do not like to show their feelings.

GEMINI (May 21 to June 20). Gemini is the third sign of the zodiac. These people are usually very intelligent and ambitious and have a great desire to learn. They can be far too critical and analytical.

You could never call them idealists; it would be hard to find a more materialistic type. Their stubborn skepticism can be annoying and they nearly always want to begin something new before finishing what they already have

Prophetic Devices

started. They like to be on the move and hate to stay in one place for any length of time.

People are inclined to think that Geminis are unreliable because of their love of change. It is indecision that makes them want a change. When they are faced with two alternatives, they may become restless and nervous, which in turn makes them a little moody.

Geminis prefer to express themselves in action rather than in words. Once their minds are made up, they can be very determined. They are successful as editors, teachers, or secretaries. They love to be kept busy; they can make extra money by doing more than one job.

You would have to show proof to convince a Gemini that something can be done successfully your way. They are usually very quick-witted with a good degree of subtlety.

Geminis born between May 21 and May 31 possess the characteristics most truly representative of this sign. Although their mental powers are highly developed, they experience constant difficulty in concentrating their attention on any one subject. Since it is their nature to be always in a state of flux and rarely to see an undertaking to its conclusion, they are generally not as successful as those born in other parts of this sign. If they do not exercise self-control, they can drift through life without achieving anything worthwhile.

June 1 to June 10 subjects usually are the most well balanced people of this sign and their critical faculties are highly developed. They struggle against the tendency to vacillate when making a decision and are almost always in firm command of their lives. For this reason, financial and social success does not easily elude this group of Geminis and it contributes to the great personal happiness that they are known to enjoy. They are less prone to mental conflict than the others of this sign since they are more readily able to adjust to their dual personality.

June 11 to June 20 subjects will always be popular. They are the great humanitarians of this sign and love people, children, and animals. They can be generous to a fault if they really believe that their actions can be of benefit to others. They are inclined to spoil children, and have been known to donate money to charity that they could not really afford. They are kindly, sociable types who would not willingly hurt anyone; similarly, they are very sensitive and make an extra effort not to be hurt. Yet they strive to give no outward indication when they are hurt or endure disappointment.

Constitutionally, Geminis do not always have great strength. They suffer from nervous exhaustion owing to their inclination to worry over the littlest things. They can suffer from bronchitis and rheumatism. Yet it is a fact that, if they look after themselves when young, they will avoid many discomforts later on in life.

"Luck-bringers" for Geminis:

The most prosperous colors for them are yellow and orange, and sometimes all shades of green.

The jewel to be worn when possible is the agate, but it is known that gold, worn without any embellishment, has the same effect for them.

The most fortunate day of the week may be either Sunday or Thursday, sometimes both.

Their lucky month is April. I would warn them to be careful in February.

In the choice of a marriage partner, they would get on extremely well with either Libran subjects (born between September 22 and October 22) or with Aquarians (born January 21 to February 18). They do not usually get along with Capricorn subjects.

Prophetic Devices

A Libran is a happy person, who is both artistic and fond of pleasure. He can be very sensitive and quite easily hurt, but is also very fair-minded and most thoughtful of others.

On the other hand, an Aquarian partner is a quiet, inoffensive person whom the Gemini may find difficult to understand at times. Try to remember that an Aquarian is inclined to the refined side of life. Never ridicule his consideration for others and try to be completely honest with him, or you will not be forgiven.

CANCER (June 21 to July 21). Cancer is the fourth sign of the zodiac and is well known for producing those who are the strongest maternal types.

These subjects usually have a great deal of feeling. They are generous, sensitive, and rather inclined to be retiring. Characteristically, they are unlike any other sign and appear absolutely peculiar to others. They are either full of rather attractive idiosyncrasies or they are absolute sticklers for convention.

They like to be in the limelight, although they do put up the facade of an unassuming attitude. But a Cancer subject does not need a lot of persuasion to come forward.

They can be very thrifty, and their wonderful gift of imagination places them in the romantic class. However, if angered, they are the most contrary. This, in turn, may cause them to be irritable and peevish unless they are able to control their tempers.

A fault of theirs is indecision and consequent hesitation. They can be extremely exasperating until they have learned to master this fault. When they wish, they are able to get their own way by willpower, perseverance, and gentle persuasion rather than by being abrupt and insistent.

Probing the Unknown

These people are either tireless and very ambitious or sluggish and lazy. They are also noted for their good memories. One thing they have in common is their love of antiques, anything of great age.

Cancerians born between June 21 and June 30 tend to be the most sensitive members of this group. If they have a goal, they pursue it with steady persistence until it is achieved. They must exercise this same diligence in not allowing others to take advantage of them.

July 1 to July 10 subjects are often the most spectacular members of this sign. Their natural attractive appearance, strong physique, and persuasive personality allow them to gain their own way with little difficulty. Malice is a possible fault in their character—they can be rather dangerous when upset—and they are inclined to be rather unforgiving by nature.

July 11 to July 21 subjects are usually the nicest group of Cancerians. They are extremely sympathetic and very kindhearted. Normally success comes to them rather late in life. They are capable of great depth in love and also intense jealousy.

Usually, Cancer subjects do very well as nurses, managers, caterers, and manufacturers. Cancer is a watery sign and most subjects are good sailors. They do very well financially at some stage in life.

Constitutionally, Cancer subjects are not the strongest. They are inclined to suffer with stomach complaints, mainly through emotional stress. Ailments that are not unknown to them are indigestion and rheumatism, and when under strain they do seem to give way, temporarily, rather easily.

The "luck-bringers" for Cancer subjects:
The colors best for them are green and gray.
The jewel is their birthstone, the ruby.

Prophetic Devices

The days of the week most fortunate for them are either Thursdays or Saturdays, but never a Monday.

Their lucky month may be either April or September.

Marriage: Cancer subjects invariably mate successfully if they select a partner from either Scorpio (born between October 23 and November 21) or Pisces (February 19 to March 20). An Arian subject (born between March 21 and April 20) is not usually a good partner for them.

With a Scorpio partner you may expect a rather dogmatic, possessive type of person whose only thought is for you and who will go to any lengths to protect you. There may also be times when you must be diplomatic in order to avoid a Scorpian's scorn for saying something wrong.

Should you choose a Pisces subject, then you can expect a very fine marriage, for Pisceans are very receptive and impressionable. They are easygoing, never very determined or very persistent, yet they are emotional. As long as you remember to give them strength whenever they are depressed (which they are inclined to be now and then), you cannot choose a better partner.

LEO (July 22 to August 21). Leo is the fifth sign of the zodiac. It is a very fixed sign that is rather fiery. Leo subjects are usually determined, faithful types whose generosity and emotions are sometimes at fault, because they appear to know no bounds whatsoever.

They are very good listeners, an asset that not many of the other signs possess, and are extremely sympathetic and helpful to others. Leo subjects are very adaptable to whatever circumstances they find themselves in, yet they can be headstrong when their feelings are aroused and consequently can be both hasty and passionate.

A Leo friend is a friend indeed, and it would be hard to

Probing the Unknown

persuade him to listen to any adverse talk about you. Leo's strongest virtues are faith and trust. If they find that their faith has been misplaced, you can be sure that they will feel very upset about this.

Leos are perfectionists and have very high goals that they find take a long while to reach. They are very open and want to share things with those they love. This is irritating to others who do not possess these attributes. You could never call them malicious; when they are wronged, at first they can be very contemptuous, but when calm they will readily forgive.

They are very self-confident and usually know exactly what they want. They always attempt to be practical in their ideas and this in turn helps them to adapt to any circumstances they may find themselves in.

They are the plodders and will keep going until they reach a goal. This is due to their strong intuitive feelings, which, more often than not, give them an advantage over others.

If you know a Leo subject well, you will probably find that he has sudden fits of depression for no accountable reason. This is because he allows his feelings to run much deeper than most.

Leo subjects are very successful as organizers, public relations officers, doctors, and managers. They like to do things for the happiness and benefit of others less fortunate than they.

Leos born between July 22 and July 31 take great pleasure in mixing socially with large groups of people. They are actually aware of their well-developed dynamic qualities and their personal power. They are the most outstanding members of this sign and are extraordinarily well balanced.

August 1 to August 10 subjects possess the greatest

self-confidence and the highest ambitions. They express their opinions with great freedom, but these outspoken characteristics often create problems for them. Yet others must be careful of this group of Leos; they love to manage or control people. They have the ability to organize, can maintain concentration on a particular point, and are entirely self-reliant. They can often rise far above the normal level of achievement for this group.

August 11 to August 21 subjects are known to be the most affectionate of this group. They can be rather impulsive at times, but they are also extremely kind and generous. Their most usual fault is a lack of patience when trying to solve a problem. They are highly charged, extremely passionate, and their personal relations with others are often deeply emotional.

Usually Leos are very cosmopolitan in their outlook and attitude.

Constitutionally, Leo subjects are invariably strong and possess more than a fair share of vitality and energy, which gives them tremendous powers of recuperation. If anything, the small of the back may give them a bit of trouble, but generally they live long healthy lives.

"Luck-bringers" for Leos:

The colors best around them are yellow and gold, and in difficult times gold would be luckier for them.

The jewel is their birthstone, the sapphire.

The day of the week best for them is either a Wednesday or Thursday, and I would advise them not to do anything important on a Monday.

The month that should bring them great happiness is March.

Marriage: Leo subjects are unlike those of other signs. They may well find the perfect mate born under any sign, with the exception of Capricornians (born December 21

Probing the Unknown

to January 19) and those born under Scorpio (October 23 to November 21). These do not normally make the best partners for a successful relationship.

VIRGO (August 22 to September 21). The celestial sign of Virgo is the sixth of the zodiac. It is a mutable sign and those born under it are usually intelligent, very methodical, and can have high powers of discrimination. At times they can be a little too critical.

Virgoans are certainly not dreamers; they are very down-to-earth and believe in doing things as matter-of-factly as possible. I do not mean that they won't believe anything they cannot see, but, being one of the strongest business-type personalities, they rarely have time to do, or even think about, anything except what is already at hand.

They are cautious, self-possessed people with an eye open for the main opportunity.

It would be rare to find extremists among Virgoan subjects, because they are very well balanced and determined; they prefer to work in a peaceful fashion, with no make-believe.

They are most discreet and genuinely prefer to be in the background and take on the atmosphere of others around them rather than create their own atmosphere.

In business they seem to have an almost psychic flair and very often find themselves prone to temptation. In most cases they are able to resist the temptations that come their way.

In business, Virgoans have no sentiment. Being commercially minded, they are successful as models, merchants, chemists, and photographers. You can be fairly certain that if you employ a Virgo subject you need not be concerned because they are very good, steady workers.

Prophetic Devices

Virgoans born between August 22 and August 31 in most cases are not given to rash decisions and acting upon impulse. They are shy, inclined to premeditation, and can be quite fussy at times. The influence of the sun on their date of birth is the factor that most affects their personality. They like to work things out carefully—often calculating the most trivial detail before they will commit themselves to a decision—and they are considered to be extremely clever. The aim for material rather than artistic success enables them to acquire wealth over a period of time, but they never squander their money. This group tends to take life quite seriously.

September 1 to September 10 subjects are highly critical of other people and of themselves and tend to be oversensitive. They meet with a great deal of success—mainly due to the way in which they reason everything out in a persistent and thorough manner. This group is certainly the most creative section of Virgo and they are endowed with marvelous imaginations. Not only do they dream but they have the ability and the willpower to make their dreams become realities. They hold a great deal of attraction for members of the opposite sex that is enhanced by their natural sensitivity to the feelings of others. This attribute is produced by the influence of Venus, the perfect matchmaker, on this section of Virgo.

September 11 to September 21 subjects lead a less active life than the other members of this sign, because they posesss the greatest degree of reserve and natural shyness. They are more prone to give way to temptation than the other groups, and possibly are inclined to be less firm when observing moral conventions. In other respects, however, they show a high degree of integrity. Mercury—the planet influence for this section—the giver of wisdom, adds favorably to their natural intelligence and determination. They seem to derive great happiness from helping others and are most at ease when in this situation.

Constitutionally, the Virgo subjects are quite strong and inclined to worry much more than any of the other signs. They are greatly influenced by those around them. They have a tendency to put on far too much weight but, by watching their diet, this need never become a serious problem.

The "luck-bringers" for Virgoans:

The best colors for them are all shades of brown, gray, and rust.

The jewel is their birthstone, the peridot.

The most fortunate day for them is a Tuesday, and they should not do anything important on a Monday.

I cannot choose a particular month for Virgoans, for good fortune and happiness are evenly spread throughout the year.

Marriage: Virgo people have quite a puritanical outlook, which could be a bit of a problem.

It has been found that for a harmonious relationship they match extremely well with those born under Capricorn (December 21 to January 19), and also those born under Taurus (April 21 to May 20). They should never marry Scorpios (October 23 to November 21) if they wish long-term happiness and contentment.

Should they choose to marry Capricorn subjects, they will find their partners very ambitious, very interested in the way other people look and dress; they are also very careful and have profound ideas. Capricornians are self-confident and at times can be insensitive to other people's feelings, because they tend to be cruel in their statements and don't think before speaking.

Should Virgoans choose to marry Taurians, they will

find great strength in this marriage partner and know that they will not be likely to be let down at any time. At the same time, the Virgoan will have to put up with a certain amount of stubborn dogmaticalness, and he must treat his partner tactfully early in the morning to avoid a demonstration of rather fierce temperament for a short period.

LIBRA (September 22 to October 22). Libra is the seventh sign of the zodiac, well balanced and belonging to the refined types who are very righteous in their actions and outlook. They are harmonious and happy people.

They possess strong artistic ability and are generous, but not stupidly so. It would be difficult to fool a Libran because his inbred intuition rarely fails him.

People like Librans because of their warm friendliness; they make very good intermediaries, for they are able to see two sides of an argument and give a neutral answer by making fair comparisons. To get the best work from a Libran, he has to be pressed, and with the right encouragement and drive he will work very enthusiastically.

Tact is one of their good points, and you will find most Librans very affable. They enjoy being the center of attraction and have a somewhat demonstrative disposition. They are able to attract their full share of affection. Because they like affection, they sometimes lack strength when it is needed.

They are very perceptive and are not easily fooled by deception. Never deceive a Libran, for he does not forgive and forget easily. You may find that you have made an enemy for life. On the other hand, they will do their utmost to protect those they love.

Librans born between September 22 and September 30 are perhaps the most impressionable and yet the most

Probing the Unknown

poised of this sign. They possess flexible minds and have very quick mental reactions; they are very adaptable and can adjust to changing circumstances with little external expression. This may cause others to think that they are not affected by change, which is not true. They are capable of being hurt and possess very deep feelings; personal relationships mean a great deal to them, as do their family ties. Members of this group respond very quickly to emotion and are sympathetic and generous in this field. They are extremely affectionate, but require the love and encouragement of those close to them to nourish their positive qualities.

October 1 to October 10 subjects possess basic humanitarian drives. They have integrity, strength, and power in equal proportions; their complete understanding of sorrow, and of suffering caused by human weakness, only serves to strengthen their resolve to alleviate the resultant unhappiness. They are excellent workers, especially if there is a worthwhile cause to pursue. But they lack personal ambition and prefer to remain in the background. Their basic fault lies in their becoming fanatical about causes and losing their sense of perspective.

October 14 to October 22 subjects are logical, very reliable, generous, and probably intellectual in their outlook. They are good companions because, being at ease themselves, friends and acquaintances find relaxation from their company. Nobody can hurry them; they will not be pushed. Members of this group don't like quarrels and will often go out of their way to be conciliatory in order to preserve the peace their nature demands. They also possess a fairly strong creative ability. Their one fault is an occasional selfishness of pride, and this will make them obstinate and rather narrow-minded. They become

Prophetic Devices

unhappy and moody at times like these, because such reactions are foreign to their basic nature.

They are most successful in the artistic field and also make very good singers, artists, designers, and personal secretaries.

Constitutionally, Librans are fairly strong and are not prone to any one particular sickness, as long as they maintain a moderate and abstemious regimen. They are able to overcome their few aches and pains more speedily than most people.

Libra is a lucky sign, but Librans do have their "luck-bringers," too:

The most advantageous colors for them are green, blue, and brown.

The jewel for them is the stone of balance, the opal.

The most fortunate days of the week for them are either Wednesdays or Saturdays, but not, in the usual run, Fridays.

The luckiest month for them is August; September does not connote good fortune for Librans.

Marriage: They seem to get along extremely well with either an Aquarian type (January 20 to February 18) or a Gemini type (May 21 to June 20).

Should they choose an Aquarian, they will find a mate of this sign to be very patient and humane, but a little difficult to understand at times, for they can be too quiet, and a little too intellectual. They are honest, but at times they tend to be a bit capricious and possessive.

On the other hand, should they select a Gemini partner, they will find him or her to be quite stubborn and not the most demonstrative of partners. Gemini subjects are extremely loyal and they believe more in deeds than in words. They are sensitive and at times appear to be a

Probing the Unknown

little unreliable because of their state of indecision. They would do almost anything for the ones they love.

SCORPIO (October 23 to November 21). Scorpio is the eighth sign of the zodiac. It is a fixed sign, and therefore its subjects are likely to be quietly controlled. Personally, they possess some attractive qualities: They are firm and yet cohesive, are extremely discreet and cautious, and must be completely sure of something before committing themselves.

Where work is concerned, they appreciate encouragement and praise, but this does not enter into their calculations when they start a job at hand.

There are two completely different types of Scorpios: One group knows exactly what to do in a job, does it competently, and is most discreet. These are very nice people as long as you don't cross them.

The other group is the opposite—inclined to be selfish and a little scheming. They work for their own benefit and are insensitive to other people's feelings when they want their own way.

Scorpio types have a good sense of judgment about people and things. They have more concealed powers than subjects of other signs. They have rather bad tempers and are inclined to be a little envious and jealous of others.

Scorpios born between October 23 and October 31 have a great sense of loyalty and are easily influenced by other people. They have a natural modesty that often keeps them contentedly in the background. Few people could accuse them of being overtalkative, and it is not always apparent that they have comprehended the point of a conversation at all. They possess the most dominant personality of this sign, but tend to hide much of their determination behind a quiet facade. These Scorpios have the potential for success in anything they attempt, and the qualities of leadership are inherent in their character.

November 1 to November 10 subjects are friendly and chatty types who tend also to be less tactful than other members of this sign. Their guileless and uncomplicated character causes them to place great confidence and trust in others. When their trust has been violated they are easily hurt. Their great personal charm and forceful powers enable them to lead and influence others. They absorb ideas with great speed and are quick to learn. Their minds are quite creative, and they have the seed of greatness in them.

November 11 to November 21 subjects are no doubt the most ambitious Scorpios. They are not likely to be deterred in their aims by their own personality flaws. Their tenacious ambition is strongest when it involves business or domestic life, although their driving determination is disguised under a deceptively gentle exterior. They have a will of iron, which usually brings them the success they crave. They want to believe the best of others and seem to be generally warmhearted and generous in their attitude. If someone betrays their confidence, however, they quickly become depressed and retaliate in a ruthless way. Their main fault is a tendency to become too proud and arrogant.

Scorpios have proved to be most successful as supervisors, policemen and policewomen, government officials, dentists, and electricians.

Constitutionally, the Scorpio types are the strongest. They do their utmost to resist any great strain before they allow themselves to give in. They seem to have a reserve of energy kept aside just for the time when it is most needed. Rheumatism and allied ailments may affect them, but not until later in life.

"Luck-bringers" for Scorpios:

The colors that give them confidence and determination are dark red and crimson.

The jewel that gives them good fortune and strength is the topaz.

The day to solve any problems is invariably a Wednesday, not at any time on a Saturday.

The most outstanding month for Scorpio subjects is February.

Marriage: For harmony and happiness in this field, it is well for Scorpio subjects to know that they mate very well with either Cancer types (June 21 to July 21) or, odd as it may be, with someone of their own sign, a Scorpio. I would advise against a Pisces (February 19 to March 20); this seldom works out.

Should they choose a Cancer mate they will find a very emotional person by nature, very sensitive and timid. They need a great deal of attention to be happy. They have to be coaxed to come forward, as they never appear to do this on their own accord. They are intelligent, and with the right treatment can be very generous. A Cancerian's characteristics are more noticeable than those of other signs, and therefore they stick to convention more closely.

SAGITTARIUS (November 22 to December 20). Sagittarius, in the ninth position of the zodiac, is a susceptible sign belonging to instinctively happy, optimistic types.

These subjects have a great deal of energy and can be extremely loyal and understanding. They have no diffi-

Prophetic Devices

culty expressing themselves and, where romance is concerned, are much more demonstrative than any of the other signs.

You could never call them conventionalists, for they believe in freedom of thought and action and will do their utmost to achieve these two things.

Unfortunately for those concerned, Sagittarians have an uncanny instinct for finding out the weak spot in another person and using it to their advantage.

It would be hard to find more open and frank types; they do not like deceit, have very high principles, and are very independent by nature.

Tidiness is not one of their best attributes; they have little regard for this. When something of importance to them comes up, they have a one-track mind.

Once a Sagittarian has made up his mind to do something, it would be unwise to try and stop him; if you do, he will turn against you and be ready for a good fight.

Sagittarians born between November 22 and November 30 have a strong spirit of rebellion that tends to reject control, convention, and authority. They are usually outspoken and extremely candid in their opinions. Their minds are often more keenly analytical than others of this sign—it would not seem strange if one of them took a watch to pieces just to satisfy his curiosity. It is possible that they will have a certain amount of trouble in their emotional relationships; they seek perfection in other people and inevitably they are bitterly disappointed when their expectations are not met. They can, of course, prevent this unhappiness with foresight and the realization that no one is perfect. However, these Sagittarians are no less sparing of themselves; they strive to contribute to life as much as is humanly possible.

December 1 to December 10 subjects are the more

Probing the Unknown

emotional types of this sign. Their natural friendliness makes them somewhat talkative at times, and they find it difficult to keep a secret. They are the most independent group of this sign and have minds that analyze and debate almost everything, but philosophical subjects have special appeal for them. They possess great vitality and personal power, which makes them extremely popular. They are a resilient group, yet they are very sensitive to outside impressions and happenings. Their uncanny sense of intuition enables them to assess a situation at a glance and take the appropriate action, which rarely results in a wrong decision. They also have a knack for drawing out the truth from people; it is difficult to tell them a lie, because of their ability to sum up any given situation almost at once in a clear and accurate manner. They are often very affectionate and are quick to make deep and lasting friendships with people they instinctively trust.

December 11 to December 20 subjects are the really determined and persevering ones in this sign. At times they devote themselves so single-mindedly to one purpose that they are accused of indifference to the feelings of others and are considered selfish. This is not usually the case, although they are quick to anger if their opinions are challenged and are apt to give someone a tongue-lashing. This group possesses natural wit but they can be sarcastic when they wish to hurt someone's feelings. Their great reserves of latent power aid them in fulfilling their ambitions for achievement. At times they are known to be rather intolerant, but in general are loyal and thoroughly trustworthy people.

The vocations in which Sagittarians are most successful are teaching and designing. They also make excellent social workers and have an aptitude for clerical duties.

Constitutionally, Sagittarians are strong. They must take it easy and not worry too much if they have chest problems. Catarrh and bronchitis are weaknesses. It is essential for Sagittarians to get as much outdoor exercise as possible.

"Luck-bringers" for Sagittarians:

The most fortunate colors for them are purple and all allied shades.

The jewel they should wear is the turquoise.

The day for important decisions is Friday, but never a Monday.

I cannot pick a particularly fortunate month because Sagittarians are able to bring important issues to a head at any time during the year.

Marriage: On the whole, Sagittarians are most successful with either an Aries (those born between March 21 and April 20) or a Libra (September 22 to October 22). There is little hope of a successful partnership with a Capricorn type.

Should the Sagittarian choose an Aries subject, he will find his mate to have a slightly explosive nature, for although he himself is rebellious, the Arian must be the leader. However, the Arian is' a perfect foil for his own independent nature and, where protection is concerned, he could not find a better partner.

On the other hand, should he choose a Libran, then a peaceful life lies ahead, and a good circle of friends. He can be quite sure that the Libran will always treat him well because Librans usually want to please; however, at times the Sagittarian may be a little bored by this.

CAPRICORN (December 21 to January 19). Capricorn is the tenth sign of the zodiac. It is a distinguished yet earthy sign of giving.

People born under Capricorn are perfectionists and are ambitious and idealistic. In appearance they are a very handsome group, and there is little to be desired.

Often they are accused of being misers, for they are very good savers. They are very profound when stating their views. Although outwardly they appear to be modest and shy, this is not so, for they have very strong determination and are to be admired for their perseverance when their minds are made up. They are very efficient about their work but must be left to do it in their own time.

You could never accuse them of being opinionated; they are friendly and strive to have people think well of them. They prefer not to be involved with other people's affairs and tend to mind their own business.

There are two different types of Capricornians: the leaders, who like to organize others, and those who like to let people know what, and how, they are doing a job and want to be known as "plodders."

Capricornians born between December 21 and December 31 are often guilty of being fickle. This is because of their tendency to be indecisive and to have rather grand ideas on too large a scale. The members of this group too often lack the determination and stamina that would enable them to finish one project before going on to something new. As a result, their fortunes have a tendency to fluctuate up and down.

January 1 to January 10 subjects are the more obstinate types of this sign. If someone says that blue is blue, they are more than ready to argue that it's really pink. They are steady, solid plodders, but often they lack the

Prophetic Devices

energy necessary to see a job right through to the end, or to reach for greatness rather than the mediocre. However, there is one big compensation—these Capricornians are extremely likable.

January 11 to January 19 subjects are the most gifted of all Capricornians. They invariably have very good brains plus extremely friendly dispositions. And, as if that weren't good enough, they are modest, too. Nine times out of ten they are able to improve their standard of living by determination and ambition. Their only failing is the inability sometimes to see the opportunities that should be painfully evident to them.

The differences between the three types are caused by the "pull" of the two signs that precede and follow Capricorn.

Those born at the beginning of this sign will automatically be affected by the preceding sign. Others born during the middle of the sign will be much more true to the characteristics of Capricorn, while those whose birthdays fall in the last period of the sign will have a slight leaning toward the sign that follows. This means that Capricornians born between December 21 and 31 will have some Sagittarian influence, those born between January 1 and 10 will be absolutely true to their birth sign, Capricorn, and those born between January 11 and 19 will automatically possess some Aquarian traits.

Normally, Capricornians are most successful as builders, air hostesses, agricultural workers, engineers, mechanics, and possibly banking consultants.

Constitutionally, the Capricornian has a great deal of strength; the only ailment inclined to bother him is depression.

"Luck-bringers" for Capricorn subjects are:

Probing the Unknown

The colors best to have around them are black and dark brown, and occasionally multiple reds give them good luck.

The jewel that will bring them the greatest happiness is the garnet. It has been found that the ruby can have the same effect for them.

The day of the week to solve any important matters is a Tuesday. They should avoid doing any important business on a Sunday.

The best time of the year for them is mid-June to mid-July.

Marriage is something Capricorn subjects do not rush into. They usually take quite a while before they make up their minds about it. It has been found that they are best suited to either a Virgo type (born between August 22 and September 21) or someone of their own sign, a Capricorn. They do not generally have a lasting partnership with a Leo type (born between July 22 and August 21).

Should they choose Virgo types, they will find them to be very generous hearted, although at times inclined to get into depressed moods. It is best to leave Virgoans alone when they are depressed, which is usually for only a short time. They can also look forward to very happy periods.

AQUARIUS (January 20 to February 18). Aquarius is the eleventh sign of the zodiac. Its members are humane, quiet, and sympathetic characters who are sometimes a little difficult to understand. Their interests are inclined toward the artistic field, and they love music and literature and are enthusiastic theatergoers. They are very studious and deep thinking by nature and are very reliable types.

Prophetic Devices

One could never say that Aquarians lack energy, for they are usually occupied with something constantly. When they have a job at hand they like to accomplish this right away, and you would be unwise to try to divert them from their purpose.

You may meet Aquarians who are selfish, unreliable, conceited, and overbearing. You can find the odd ones in all of the signs. But, on the whole, you will find Aquarians to be kind and sympathetic to those they know. They carry on quietly with their aims and have a genuine ambition to better themselves. They put anyone they love on a very high level.

Aquarians born between January 20 and January 31 are noted for their ability to use their intelligence to the greatest advantage. They are extremely alert to any happening around them and enjoy painstaking study and research. They are generally extremely courteous, polite, and kind to a fault, and are extremely well disciplined. They like to study a subject carefully and have a wide range of interests and exceptional general knowledge.

February 1 to February 10 subjects are almost the exact opposite. Obedience is certainly not one of their assets and they find it difficult to trust other people. They can be extremely suspicious and are often left wide open to disappointment. Because of this natural distrust, they can miss opportunities that should be obvious to them. They do not give their hearts or their help easily.

February 11 to February 20 subjects have the ability to penetrate to the heart of a situation or problem. They are generally people really worth knowing and befriending, and their natural generosity falls easily on those around them. The members of this group are often the most artistic of their sign and are dedicated to the arts. They undertake anything with wholehearted dedication

Probing the Unknown

and they pour into it all of their effort and concentration.

Most Aquarians like efficiency, and they find it difficult to suffer fools around them.

Constitutionally, Aquarians do not have a great deal of strength. An ailment that may cause them discomfort is rheumatism; their circulation frequently leaves much to be desired. However, if they take care of themselves in youth, they will not suffer too greatly in later life.

"Luck-bringers" for Aquarians:

The colors best suited for them are usually blacks or blues.

The jewel they should wear whenever possible is their birthstone, the amethyst.

The most successful day of the week for them is either a Monday or a Thursday.

The best month may be any one of the following—June, September, or October—but never April or May.

Marriage: Aquarians do not rush into marriage; they give it a lot of thought. When they do marry, they make very loyal and attentive partners. They have been known to have great happiness with either Geminis (born between May 21 and June 20) or Librans (born between September 22 and October 22).

Should the choice be a Gemini, they can expect to find a very intelligent yet often an extremely stubborn person. It may be wise sometimes to impart an idea so skillfully that the Gemini thinks it's his own. Then the idea will be accepted with enthusiasm. Encouragement and praise will keep the Gemini very happy.

On the other hand, should an Aquarian choose a Libran subject, he may be in for some irritating times. Librans are inclined to overdo being fair and just. They can be overgenerous at times, at the cost of their loved ones.

Any deceit is best owned up to with a Libran, for he or she will forgive readily, but if you do not own up, beware if you are found out.

PISCES (February 19 to March 20). Pisces is the twelfth and last sign of the zodiac. Subjects of this sign are easily impressed because they are extremely receptive and consequently can make successful mediums. While they are persistent, they are rarely positive in their actions, and their emotions are apt to make them easily influenced by other people.

At times, when they are depressed, no matter how small the problem may be, they can sink to a very low level. When they are without cares, they are wonderful company, extremely kind and generous. Show a Piscean an underdog and he will do whatever he can on that person's behalf. Pisceans are usually animal lovers, too.

When the Piscean is depressed, he is very quiet, keeps it all to himself, and does not take it out on those around him. Where finances are concerned he is quite flexible, inasmuch as one minute he will save every penny and the next will happily spend money like water. Being a dual sign (the fishes), the subjects can show two extreme sides of their character at the same time.

Pisceans will take on heavy responsibilities as long as they know it is worthwhile. They do not like failures and will put forward a strong front when they really are not sure of something.

Pisceans born between February 19 and 29 are likely to be the most ambitious of this sign and like to be recognized for their better qualities. They often miss opportunities in life because they always show such extreme caution; this characteristic can thwart their per-

Probing the Unknown

sonal ambitions, because they don't like to take chances in life.

March 1 to March 10 subjects frequently have to endure domestic worries, which are invariably brought about by their own temperaments. They tend to live in a world of their own at times, and good fortune in many instances eludes them.

March 11 to March 20 subjects are likely to display the greatest confidence in themselves. They are apt to possess a good opinion of their own capabilities, but are not always realistic in their approach to other people. They have keen analytical minds and will probe deeply into a matter that is not easily understood. They tend to be among the most restless of all Pisceans, but on the whole are nice people who make good friends.

It has been found that Pisceans are successful as caterers, nurses, teachers, and fashion leaders. They like jobs that they feel will benefit others less fortunate than they.

Constitutionally, Pisceans are fairly strong. As long as they avoid extremes and keep to a regular pattern of life and diet, they will be able to keep a good record of all-around health. Disorders of the blood are the one thing that may trouble them most.

"Luck-bringers" for Pisceans:

The best colors for them are blue, purple, and mauve.

The jewel they should wear whenever possible is their birthstone, the bloodstone.

The day of the week to solve any important problems is either Tuesday or Saturday.

I cannot single out the luckiest month of the year for Pisceans, because good fortune is evenly distributed throughout the year, with slightly more favorable indications during the early months.

Marriage: It has been found that Pisceans get along extremely well with Cancer subjects (June 21 to July 21) or with Scorpions (born between October 23 and November 21).

Should their choice be a Cancer subject, they will find a very career-conscious person who has a good sense of humor. At times a Cancerian can be very stubborn, but when he is persuaded in the right way his generosity knows no bounds.

However, should a Piscean choose a Scorpio mate, he can expect a very devoted person who may be a little too possessive. This type will do the utmost for the good and protection of his mate. If you try to harm the Scorpio's mate in any way, you will certainly know what you are up against.

Try not to make impulsive statements to Scorpios, for they have excellent memories, especially when slighted. Also, remember that if you wish the Scorpio subject to do something your way, it is best to discuss the matter quietly and sensibly, rather than in anger, which will accomplish nothing for you.

Astrology and Mating (Sex)

Astrology imparts an exceptionally good understanding of the feelings of others and the temptations that may be met under a given birth sign. It makes its subjects very aware of latent talents and the ability to be able to develop and make the fullest use of them to insure a happier, richer, and much fuller life. It educates you to know when you have a fortunate time and prepares you to take the fullest advantage of opportunities in situations such as meeting people whom you want to attract ro-

Probing the Unknown

mantically, in business, or socially. It also teaches you self-restraint so that you can save yourself from both hardships and heartaches.

Very often I have been asked, "Whom should I marry, or cohabit with, in order to be happy myself and give great happiness and satisfaction to my mate?" Well, as you possibly are aware, any sign has more than one of the other signs with whom it mates well. I shall discuss this later in the chapter, but first let me tell you who, from the signs, are usually given to being very hot-blooded, in other words, very sexy.

ARIES

The Arian invariably is very sexy and, whether woman or man, usually prefers to be the active person in the cohabitation. Thus the Arian has to find a person who loves him or her enough to be passive and completely understanding.

TAURUS

Taurians, especially when born after May 9, have enormous sexual appetites but, unfortunately, in many cases they do not pick well and bring upon themselves, throughout their lives, some unhappiness in this direction. It does not matter that their sexual appetites can be appeased, because their whole being, both mental and physical, may not necessarily be in complete coordination.

GEMINI

Quite often one will find that the Gemini-born are not too sex conscious. They like to be loved, but in many cases sex becomes secondary to their mental appreciation of their partner, other than when they wish to reproduce.

Prophetic Devices

Of course a Gemini has to be extremely cautious whom he selects as a partner.

CANCER

Cancer folk are sensitive people and need awakening in sex. Once this has occurred, they can be quite demanding of their mates. Bear in mind that Cancerians love children and usually reproduce on a higher scale than other signs.

LEO

While we know that Leo is supposed to be the king of the jungle, members of this sign nearly always need someone to bolster up their thoughts and feelings in most respects except in the act of sex. They want a regular routine in this direction, but not necessarily with great frequency because, as Leo people do nothing by halves, they can reap great satisfaction on the occasion of the act.

VIRGO

Virgo types are sometimes misguided about sex. As is the case with most of us, they like to be loved, and love very deeply in return. They are not the most passionate of people but they will usually cooperate in this direction with the hope of pleasing and keeping their opposite number happy. I am not necessarily saying here that they do not enjoy sex, because all healthy people do, no matter what their sign. Yet their thoughts are aimed more to please their partner than themselves.

LIBRA

Librans as a rule like to prove themselves strong-minded, and they can, when necessary, deny themselves.

Probing the Unknown

They invariably have three or four children and suddenly decide to have no more, but they are among the signs that have exceptionally healthy sexual appetites.

SCORPIO

Scorpios are possessive and are rarely passive; they never forget or forgive too easily. They are most of the time devoted to one person and it is rare to find a Scorpio having sexual affairs on the side with all and sundry.

SAGITTARIUS

Sagittarians, similar to Taurians, have happy, optimistic natures, but also in most cases have tempers to match. Therefore their sexual demands upon their partners will be, like those of the Taurian and Arian, a little more than average.

CAPRICORN

Capricornians are fiery in their sexual demands only when they are deeply in love. Basically, they are very business-minded and can go for quite long periods satisfying themselves in this direction by working hard, driving a car very fast, or playing hard, which in many cases satisfies passions. As I have said, when in love they do make constant demands.

AQUARIUS

Aquarians love the arts, music, theater, and literature and are usually fairly cosmopolitan in their outlook. By nature, they can be extremely loyal to one person in particular, yet they appear to have a great deal of affection in their bodies, enough for more than one person. They may not be inclined to stray mentally, but they will give way at times physically. The act of sex is very necessary in order to keep their minds working freely, and quite often the Aquarian looks upon this act for relief, which to his or her way of thinking usually means no more than washing one's hands. If this person's opposite number can always turn a blind eye in this direction, he or she can find no better or more loyal mate. This of course does not necessarily apply to every Aquarian.

PISCES

The Piscean usually is gifted with an extremely friendly personality and is very popular and in great demand, but, bearing in mind that the symbol of the Piscean sign is the fish, they are not the most sexual of people. Therefore, there will be occasions when their partners will almost have to ask them to cooperate in this direction, and very often the partner will become slightly suspicious, or even jealous of them, since Pisceans mix so well and so freely with others. But the partner should know that, in most cases, he or she has the most loyal and true person as a mate.

I am now going to give you a short guide of who, experience has taught us, mates best with whom.

ARIANS (March 21 to April 20) would do well to select their partners from Leo (July 21 to August 21) or from Gemini (May 21 to June 20), but in many cases for great peace of mind they could also select a Pisces (February 19 to March 20), bearing in mind that the Arian is usually bound to be the active person.

TAURIANS (April 21 to May 20) are ideally suited

Probing the Unknown

should they elect to mate with a Capricorn (December 21 to January 19) or a Virgo (August 22 to September 21).

GEMINI (May 21 to June 20) with little doubt should select a partner where possible from Leo (July 21 to August 21) or Aquarius (January 20 to February 19).

CANCER (June 21 to July 20) mates so well with Scorpio (October 23 to November 20), and oddly enough usually does select someone from this sign. Cancerians can get along well with Pisces (February 19 to March 20), but not as well as with Scorpio.

LEO (July 21 to August 21), being such an adaptable sign, can usually mate very well with most signs other than Capricorn or Scorpio. But, it appears from experience, their best selection should come from Gemini (May 21 to June 20) for lasting happiness.

VIRGOANS (August 22 to September 21) appear to mate quite well with a Capricorn (December 21 to January 19), or equally well with a Taurian (April 21 to May 20). While they may at times be attracted physically to a Scorpio (October 23 to November 20), they would make a great mistake to form a permanent association with anyone born under this sign.

LIBRANS (September 22 to October 22) should select to marry, and spend their days with happiness and satisfaction, from either an Aquarian (January 20 to February 19) or an Arian (March 21 to April 20).

SCORPIOS (October 23 to November 20) appear to mate extremely well with Cancer subjects (June 21 to July 20), or in some cases other Scorpios.

SAGITTARIANS (November 21 to December 20) should select a partner from Aries (March 21 to April 20) or from Libra (September 22 to October 22), be-

Prophetic Devices

cause at times this sign likes a slightly explosive atmosphere. A Sagittarian will obtain this and would also find great protection with an Arian or a Libran.

CAPRICORNIANS (December 21 to January 19) are invariably best suited to either Virgo (August 22 to September 21) or to Capricorn. There have been rare occasions when a Capricornian has been known to mate well with someone born under the sign of Scorpio (October 23 to November 20).

The AQUARIAN (January 20 to February 18) appears to get very great happiness from either a Gemini (May 21 to June 20) or a Libran (September 22 to October 22). Do not forget that the Aquarian, while enjoying sex, will also demand a high degree of intelligence from a mate.

The PISCEAN (February 19 to March 20) can have a successful union with a Cancer (June 21 to July 20), and on occasion with an Arian (March 21 to April 20). When the decision is to mate with an Arian, the result appears to be excellent for both signs.

Dice

Another prophetic device that has been used over the years is dice. In order to foretell your future, you use three dice, shake these well in your hand, or, better still, in a canister, and then throw them out onto a table.

You must always add the complete value of the three dice that you have thrown. For example: If you threw three ones, then this would become three; three sixes would automatically become eighteen.

Whatever number you throw should indicate to you the way things are going or are about to go for you.

Probing the Unknown

Here is a list of all possible die totals obtained by throwing the three dice and my readings for these various combinations:

3. This means that you are either entering into a good period or can expect an unlooked-for, yet pleasing, gift.
4. This represents the likelihood that caution is necessary, for you could be dealing with someone who will be rather difficult.
5. You can expect to meet a new person who, in time, should prove to be a great friend and who will be advantageous in your life for a long period.
6. This warns you to keep your eye on personal things around you or even on someone of whom you are fond, because it sometimes means that there is dishonesty nearby.
7. Chatter is indicated here. You have someone around you who has a very loose tongue, so be careful to whom you divulge your confidences.
8. You have been either a little wrong or at fault in your approach to someone, and you could be on the receiving end of a reprimand.
9. This number means a festivity, especially in the romantic field; this could be either a wedding or an engagement.
10. You will soon be hearing news of a birth; if you yourself are pregnant at the time of throwing the dice, then the number not only tells you that you will have a healthy child, but that it will be a boy.
11. This number is never a happy one, for, from experience, it has proved to indicate that either you or someone close to you will be saddened.
12. Usually this means that a cable, express letter, or urgent telephone call is coming your way.

Prophetic Devices

13. Depression and worry are suggested here, but this is not always the case. It can also indicate that you are worrying unduly.
14. For the eligible, this usually means a new romantic interest in your life, while for the married, it indicates that your partner will be proud of you for something you have achieved.
15. This warns you not to get caught up in a quarrel or thoughtless chatter with people who could involve you in an unfortunate manner.
16. Travel of an enjoyable nature is usually indicated here.
17. This is a happy number; while you are going to be extremely busy, you are at the same time going to be on the move from place to place, and there could be a change of residence for you.
18. This is the luckiest number of all to throw, for it indicates a good financial position ahead, a promotion, fortunate dividends, and great advancement in life for you.

Personal Features

Eyes

You have read here many times that I make a point of just looking into a person's eyes during my readings. You may wonder, apart from the mental pictures that I see, just what else I get from those eyes.

Herewith, for your guidance, is a short guide of the characteristics of people according to the color of their eyes:

Gray: Determined people who have strong minds,

Probing the Unknown

quarrelsome if you upset the ones they love. Emotional to the point of bringing trouble to themselves. Very hard workers.

Blue: These subjects can often be quite tough, almost to the point of being sadistic. They can be very strong, but also, on occasion, very weak. The women will be determined to obtain their own way whenever possible, and if they also have very thin lips, then take care—there are no ends they will not seek to harm you if upset. If the eyes are very pale blue, they can be sadistic on occasions, also rather sexy.

Blue Gray: Usually kind folk who will give you the world if they love you. They can be stubborn, yes, but they will yield a point when they are proved wrong. In many cases, the women who possess blue gray eyes dominate their husbands. They invariably have an extremely good sense of humor, but also a quick temper.

Hazel: The strongest point here is loyalty. It can be taken to a point of folly when reciprocated. However, if these people are crossed, they are not vicious but are apt to remember an injustice. Yet they are gifted with good common sense and are invariably nice people to know.

Brown: Extremely generous people in most cases; can be stubborn and will argue at times; but the odd mixture of simplicity and shrewdness is often a great help to them. They appear to use up more energy than most people and are extremely affectionate. While they are very loyal, they do have rather quick tempers at times.

Prophetic Devices

Green: One could call these the eyes of artists; the best dancers and singers, the best actresses and actors and painters, invariably come from this group. Women with green eyes can be both possessive and jealous. Bear in mind that green-eyed people usually have big tempers when upset. Therefore, in the normal course of things, they invariably live on their nerves.

Facial Features

When I look into a person's eyes, at the same time I naturally take in most of his other features. Over the years one learns how to judge a person not only by his eyes, but also by his ears, nose, mouth, and so on.

I thought that you might be interested in knowing what judgments I have made and in trying to see if you can, in turn, attempt reading a face.

THE NOSE

If a person has a long, aquiline-type nose, he has a good opinion of himself and is confident in many respects. He also takes things rather seriously and works with great responsibility. In quite a few cases this type of person is a conventionalist; he is not the best business type, but he usually makes money later in life.

The normal-sized nose with wide nostrils connotes an ambitious worker with original ideas. He possesses a temper if pushed too far and usually makes a big success in life in whatever field he follows. He has a good sense of humor and enjoys the good things of life.

A person who has a short nose is usually fickle by nature. He can be quite popular, but usually does not like too much responsibility. He gets along well with the opposite sex and invariably has a warm nature. But he can be a spendthrift and not a saver.

The small, narrow nose normally belongs to artistic folk who are very popular but who do procrastinate in things rather a lot. They are very loyal, but do not be fooled by their apparent friendliness, for they usually make fairly tough business people.

Those who possess flat noses are kindly, happy people, but are slow to learn, since their intelligence is good but not great. They can be most loyal—but I warn you, do not upset these people too much or you could live to regret it.

The nicely shaped nose belongs to people who, whether men or women, dress to perfection, love music and drama and anything to do with the arts. These folks can, at times, be rather critical of the imperfections of others.

THE MOUTH

A happy-looking mouth, appearing to smile most of the time, connotes a friendly, intelligent person who is gentle but can, when the occasion demands, be as firm as the next man. This characteristic seems to create a magnetic appeal in the person.

The mouth that has very thin lips usually belongs to someone who can be critical and very firm, cruel at times to the point of sadism, and on occasion both crafty and sly. It can also indicate a rather changeable nature.

Those people with thick-lipped mouths are practical, rather reserved at times, and generous when the occasion suits them. They enjoy the good things of life and have good appetites in most directions. Later in life they can suffer from blood pressure problems unless they lead an abstemious existence.

The full-lipped mouth in most instances belongs to warm and kindhearted people who are quite efficient in their work, possess strong personalities, usually mind their own business, and are loyal friends.

The person who has a small mouth most often likes to get his own way. He can be quite sweet, but could not be regarded as a strong-minded person. He does not like to have to concentrate too deeply and can be rather emotional at times. He rarely supports others, preferring to be supported, and loves to be spoiled.

The people who possess a large mouth have large outlooks and desires. They love their food and usually have a bigger than usual sex appetite. They do things in a big way, like to live opulently, and can be quite daring, but they appear to make good headway in business; it is their domestic life that they have to watch because this can be stormy at times.

THE CHIN

A rather square chin that protrudes slightly is a characteristic of very determined folk; they make headway and are not very concerned whether they please or offend in their efforts. They make wonderful friends, yet only a few because they are usually loyal to one person. Do not attempt to cross them, or you could well be the loser.

Where you see a pointed chin with an oval-shaped face, you usually find that these people are artistic, musical, sensitive folk. They can also be professors or learned people and are known to be irritatingly vague.

The person with a normal round chin can be quite easy to live with, determined, but not necessarily stubborn. You can find good average workers and devoted family folk in this category. If a strong jawline comes with the round chin, it denotes a pioneer who sticks very much to his intentions once his mind is made up.

THE EARS

Average-shaped and average-sized ears with large lobes in most cases belong to the big-minded person who has sharp vision, a good imagination, is ambitious and sympathetic. Quite a lot of psychics have this type of ear.

People with ears that appear to have no lobes, because the bottom of the ear seems to go flush with the side of the neck, have tempers and are very energetic almost to a point of being aggressive. They usually make a success in life because they have a strong sense of their responsibilities.

Small-eared people are artists, interior decorators, and creative people. They are at most times popular, but they do procrastinate, and in some cases can be considered to be weak willed. They have a strong sense of imagination, and writers can come from this group.

The large, wide-shaped ear belongs to courageous, masculine people who are not always the best conversationalists. They make good friends in a dogged type of way, but feel an emotional hurt rather deeply. Usually this type has difficulty summoning up initiative.

THE FOREHEAD

The average-sized forehead with a good hairline forming almost a widow's peak is regarded as showing a person of average intelligence but with shrewd powers of observation. I would say that this person has the patience to be able to persevere and can make fairly good headway in life. He lacks confidence at times because he is self-

Prophetic Devices

conscious. This is not an asset, for there are periods when it will hold him back from realizing his ambition.

A forehead that has good depth, one could almost say a high forehead, invariably belongs to shrewd, intelligent, and deep-thinking people. They appear both to have and to use a lot of energy and can be almost dynamos where work is concerned. It is rare for these people not to make a great success in the business field. Their observation of others is extremely good, and if they have a fault at all, it is that they do not bear fools easily.

An oval-shaped face with a high forehead can indicate an impatient, selfish person who can be rather indifferent to the feelings of others, yet would be surprised if told that this was the case. These people are very intelligent but nothing must get in their way once they are aiming at a goal; therefore they are often regarded as hard-hearted.

A good-looking forehead, which could be regarded as low and, because of the hairline, narrow, is a characteristic of someone who has a large ego but is irresponsible, is often self-conscious and intelligent, and can be evasive in a pleasant manner, but on the other hand can also be quite brutal on occasion. Lawyers and politicians sometimes have this type of forehead.

A forehead appearing to be slightly unbalanced, because there is more hair to one side than the other, usually belongs to people who do not at all times tell the truth. They are opportunists and will go to any lengths to gain their ends. They often will not even discriminate sexually. Some people who read faces will even go so far as to say that this type of person can be criminally delinquent.

3.
Dream Interpretations

It has been said by many authorities that dreams are, in effect, prophetic experiences, and intensive studies are being conducted now, as they have been for centuries, concerning their value.

There are many times, after we have fallen asleep, when our mind and our nerves are still awake. Have you not seen your pet cat or dog lying asleep but whimpering or barking and moving his legs as though in motion? Have you ever awakened quite suddenly, realizing you had been dreaming, and then tried to go back to sleep to recapture the dream? This, of course, is usually impossible. Nightmares are still another aspect of dreams and are usually frightening and vivid experiences that can leave a person in a state of agitation for a considerable period. In fact, in some cases the nightmare is so deep, so compelling in its vividness, that the dreamer has difficulty

Dream Interpretations

getting back to reality. (This is a frequent occurrence among children—sometimes intensified after a moving experience such as a serious illness or an operation or separation from loved ones.)

Quite often people experience what I term mixed-up dreams that are such a conglomeration of different things they cannot possibly mean too much; some experts claim that these can be brought about by indigestion. Other dreams, in which we participate but which we cannot recall, in my opinion stem from impressions received the day before. It is the dreams that stand out very clearly the next morning, or for days to come in our waking hours, that we should take strong note of, because these can contain either warnings, guidance for the future, or messages for us.

Since every one of us is to a certain degree psychic, I also believe that our psychic powers can be used to study and interpret our dreams. We appear to have instincts for good, and bad, even in our sleeping hours, so let us accept the fact that dreams can give us advice on how to handle people or situations. They can give us warnings and they can also bolster our ambitions, thus enabling us to go forward with great strength of mind.

In the following pages I am providing a short list of some of the major things about which one might possibly dream. I can only go by my own experiences in this area, so you will have to arrive at your own conclusions. However, I feel certain that if you consult this index it should, in most ways, coincide with events that are happening around you according to your dream.

ANCHOR   This usually is a steadying symbol. If you see it lying on dry land, it indicates that peace of mind and security will be yours. On the other hand, should the anchor be submerged in water, you can expect a few frustrations and delays.

ANGER — Usually a good dream, because you reverse its actual meaning. Either it indicates that a person close to you is very genuine and loyal or, should you know the person you are angered with in the dream, it indicates pleasing news in the very near future.

ANIMAL — It is not always good to dream about an animal, because this can mean either that you are going to make an enemy or that you are debasing yourself. Only the horse in a dream is a favorable indication for you. On the other hand, should the horse be excited, it means you are going to be successful but can expect to encounter a few business difficulties.

APPLES — If you see an apple or apples in your dream, this is extremely good, provided you are not eating them. Should you, on the other hand, be eating them, then you could be due for a few disappointments.

ARGUMENT — A warning for you to avoid entering into quarrels or arguments with others around you.

ATTIC — This has been said to mean that you are aiming high and are right to do so.

Dream Interpretations

AUTOMOBILE This can be an indication of your health or of certain physical conditions affecting parts of your body. Should you be driving the car, then you would be in fairly good health. If someone else is driving the car, then usually you are in an unwell state. Either way, to dream of an automobile does signify that you should take more care and rest.

BALCONY Whether you are standing on the balcony or others are, this is not the most cheerful sign. It can be interpreted to mean that others are standing in your way and therefore you may have to face up to a few problems.

BAPTISM This is indicative of good luck and a fresh start by means of an opportunity granted to you.

BEAUTY To dream of beauty is favorable, because it suggests that your mind is properly oriented. However, if you dream that you yourself are beautiful, then this can be taken as a warning that you are being too self-confident.

BED Should you be putting on fresh linen and making up a bed, this could mean either an engagement or marriage in the future for you. Should you be in a hotel in your dream and the bed is strange to you, this denotes that frustrations and difficulties you have been going through should now take a turn for the better.

BIBLE — To dream of the Bible is indicative of your being right and on the true path, whether it be about a person or business.

BLOOD — This is never a good dream, because it can portend disappointments, quarrels, or even a separation from someone you love dearly.

BOOKS — To dream of books that you are reading or buying is excellent, because it signifies great future happiness, and the more books you can see in your dream the better the promise.

BREAD — This shows great contentment, and if you are eating bread in your dream, then your health is going to be extremely good.

BRUSH OR BROOM — To dream about either of these things indicates something you have required or desired for quite a while should now definitely come your way.

CAKE — If the cake you see in your dream is either a birthday, wedding, or anniversary cake, this denotes that your circumstances are going to be very successful and happy, and that your health will also be good.

Dream Interpretations

CANDLE — If you are able to light a candle that you see in your dreams, and it burns clearly, this portends prosperity for you. Should you find it difficult to get the candle to light, however, you must be on your guard against troubles around you.

CARPET — If the carpet you dream about is luxurious, then you are going to be extremely fortunate. In the event that the carpet is covered by another rug or has a protective shield on top of it, you would be well advised not to let other people take advantage of you.

CERISE — To dream that you have anything the color of cerise is merely indicative of passion.

CHAIN — If the chain you see in your dream is of an exceptionally heavy type, something that has been worrying you should turn out satisfactorily. On the other hand, should you be wearing a gold or silver chain around your neck or wrist, this is usually a sign that you will receive a gift from someone who admires you greatly.

CIGARETTE — To dream that you have given a cigarette or a light for your own cigarette suggests that you can expect to receive help from someone in a new venture you are contemplating.

Probing the Unknown

CLOCK — If the clock you see in your dream is quiet, then it means that your everyday affairs are going to go quietly according to routine. In addition, if the clock is chiming, then this is very fortunate, and the louder the chime or strike, the more favorable are the indications for you.

DANGER — This is a dream in which you reverse the meaning. The more danger you see, the greater will be your success in your present surroundings. But if you see yourself just missing danger, then take this as a slight warning.

DENTIST — To dream that you are paying a visit to your dentist signifies you should take extra caution where your health is concerned, because you could be feeling unwell.

DEVIL — If you see the devil in your dream, it indicates frustrations that could last quite a while unless you take extra care.

DIAMOND — This is not an auspicious dream, for it means you can expect slight domestic upheavals to come your way.

DIVING — To dream that you are diving into water is a warning to avoid any unnecessary risks or gambles, because it is a sign that you would lose.

DUCK — To dream of a duck indicates good

fortune, always providing the duck is not pecking you. Should this be the case, then you should be aware that someone around you is being deceitful, and you should take appropriate precautions.

DUSTING If you are dusting pieces of furniture, it is fortunate. Invariably this dream indicates that you have a struggle going on around you and that it will now be starting to work out well for you.

EARTH If the earth is parched or dried up, you are not being honest with yourself and are being extravagant; you must try to put this right. But if the earth, as you envision it, contains rich soil, then very happy times are in store for you.

ECSTASY Ecstasy usually signifies you are not concentrating sufficiently; if you make a strong effort in this direction, then affairs should improve.

EGG It is a good sign if the egg or eggs you see in your dream are perfect, because the more you see, the greater will be your worldly possessions. On the other hand, should your egg be broken or cracked, this could indicate dishonesty, a loss, or burglary.

ELEPHANT An elephant suggests power and might. If the elephant is picking you up, it denotes a promotion for you. If the elephant is trying to avoid you, it indicates you have someone in your circle who is cunning and devious.

EMERALDS — Emeralds given to you portend that you need to take extra care about someone who is very close to you.

ENTERTAIN-MENT — This is a lucky dream if you are enjoying yourself. Should you put someone else off in order to attend a party, it indicates that you are going to be able to grasp an opportunity that is coming your way. On the other hand, should you wish to attend a party and cannot make it, you could lose a good opportunity because of the bad behavior of someone around you.

EVIL — Although it is not a bad omen to dream of evil, it means that someone does not wish you well; you should therefore keep your eyes open where your working life is concerned.

EXPLOSION — While this is not a bad subject to dream about, you could expect to hear some unsettling or unhappy news about someone a distance away of whom you think highly.

EYES — If the eyes of the person you are dreaming about are particularly outstanding, this denotes good fortune for you and means that a change you have been waiting to make should now come about. Should it be your own

Dream Interpretations

eyes you are dreaming about, and they are aching or you have gotten something in your eye, then someone around you is not being entirely truthful to you about things.

FAME This is a warning of bad luck coming your way, regardless of whether you are famous or someone around you has become famous.

FAT To dream that you are fat or obese is not fortunate. It is even more unlucky if the dreamer is a woman.

FEAR If you are alarmed or frightened, it means just the opposite; you are courageous and are going to be happy.

FIRE Fire portends irritations and quarrels, but if in your dream you are able to put the fire out, it denotes that some news you expect, and are pessimistic about, should turn out to be much better than you anticipated.

FISH If you or someone you know catches a fish, this is indicative of a false friend. If you see a fish swimming in clear water, it is a sign that most of what you are doing should turn out well, and that good fortune is coming your way.

FLOWERS Picking flowers suggests the loyalty of your friends. If you are throwing flowers away, a quarrel will ensue

Probing the Unknown

with someone in the near future. Nevertheless, flowers usually mean sincerity and happiness.

FOOD — Preparing a meal and then eating it with enjoyment is extremely lucky; it means that you are going to be very satisfied with the outcome of plans you have made.

FRUIT — If a pregnant woman dreams of fruit, and sees an apple among the fruit, it is most likely that she will have a male child. Berries, however, connote annoyances and disappointments.

GAINS — Gains made through your income, or in any other direction, are a portent that you should exercise caution because someone you know is either going to cheat you or deceive you.

GARDEN — Your presence in a nicely kept garden points to luck in financial matters.

GEMS — Whether you are wearing the gems or looking at them does not foreshadow good fortune for you.

GIFT — When you are given a gift and you recognize the person who gives it to you, you would be advised not to trust that person completely, for he is being devious and conniving.

GLOOM — If you find yourself very depressed or in the depths of gloom, you can ex-

Dream Interpretations

pect an opportunity for advancement to be offered to you, and you should grasp it without hesitation.

GRIEF — This is a dream in reverse. It indicates a lot of laughter and joy coming your way.

GUN — A gun being fired means you can expect to hear news that someone is ill, but if you yourself are firing that gun, the portents are that you should take more care, for you could be the one who is sick.

HAIR — The interpretation varies according to the condition of the hair you see in your dream. If you are worried about its looks and condition, it suggests that you must concentrate more in order to get over difficulties that may be going on around you. If, on the other hand, the hair looks healthy and is well groomed, then your future prospects should be very successful.

HANDKER-CHIEF — If you are looking for a handkerchief in your dream, you can expect a very pleasing gift in the near future, and will find it easily. Should the handkerchief be difficult to find, this could mean that someone close to you may have to take a journey without you for a period.

HEART — Holding someone in high esteem who has good intentions toward you points

	to a great deal of genuine affection coming your way.
HIDING	Whether you are hiding from someone or trying to hide from something in the dream, you can expect that some rather annoying news will come to you.
HILL	The meaning varies according to the progress you make. If your progress is slow, this indicates obstacles ahead in your life, and this is the wrong period for you to try to beat them. Should you find yourself climbing your hill with great ease, then you will surmount obstacles around you, and changes and good fortune lie ahead for you.
HONOR	To dream that either you alone or someone near to you is receiving an honor should be taken as a warning that you must be rather careful and should economize more.
HORSESHOE	If you see a horseshoe lying open end up, this suggests a long journey across water. If, on the other hand, you find a horseshoe, or have one given to you as a gift, the meaning is that you could receive an inheritance in time.
INCOME	Be careful, because this is not favorable if you are trying to make extra money in order to increase your income.

Dream Interpretations

INFANT — Should you dream that you have a child who is unwell, this is a slight warning that a few annoyances could be in store for you. On the other hand, if you are looking after that child and the child is unhappy, then it is an extremely fortunate dream.

INJURY — If you yourself are the person who has been hurt, then this dream warns you to exercise caution. Should it be someone you know who is injuring you, it suggests that you would be well advised to keep your own confidence where this particular person is concerned, because momentarily you cannot trust him.

INSULT — This could have two meanings: A change could be coming your way either at home or at work. Or a few difficulties could be lying in your path that may require considerable effort to surmount.

INVALID — It is all according to how the invalid is progressing in your dream. For example, should he be having a struggle to get better, then you have still a few obstacles to be overcome in your everyday life. On the other hand, should he be getting better quickly, then the portents are that the surmounting difficulties you experienced recently are abating and you will attain much greater peace of mind.

Probing the Unknown

IRONING — To dream that you see yourself ironing or smoothing things out means that you are going forward to better times and will get much greater cooperation from those who are nearest and dearest to you.

ITCHING — This is a propitious dream if you are scratching yourself because you are itchy. It indicates that you are worrying about things quite unnecessarily.

JAIL — It is a slight warning of ill health to dream that you or someone you know is either in or visiting a jail.

JARS — If you are filling a jar in your dream, the fuller your jar is, the greater will be your good luck. Even if the jar or jars are empty, this is always thought to be a very lucky dream.

JEOPARDY — Jeopardy signifies great good fortune and opportunities coming your way.

JEWELS — All jewels are considered to be very lucky, whether you are giving or receiving them in your dream, but there are exceptions. See also Diamonds, Emeralds, and Gems.

JILTING — If you have been jilted in the dream and find yourself worried and upset because of this, it is a strong sign of how very genuine the person of your choice will prove himself or herself to be.

Dream Interpretations

JOURNEY — When you dream that you are going on a long or short journey, you can expect changes in your present way of living.

JUMPING — Your jumps can symbolize difficulties you may have to meet. Should you find yourself jumping clear, then you have no need to worry because all will be well for you.

KETTLE — As long as the water in the kettle is not boiling furiously or boiling over, a kettle is indicative of good luck, but if it should be boiling over, then there could be a loss of something or someone you treasure.

KEY — A key augurs a change of home for you, but if you lose the key in your dream this is not considered fortunate.

KICK — To be on the receiving end of a kick warns you that you have a rather sadistic enemy. Should you yourself be kicking someone it is a good indication for you.

KING — To be on good terms with a king, or to have a king act nice to you, indicates a period of extremely good luck, because dreams of royalty always signify good fortune.

KISS — To dream that you are kissing a stranger, or even someone you know only slightly, is not propitious, for it warns you to be more cautious in relation to happenings going on around you.

KNEE If someone admires your knees, the connotation is lucky. Should you find that you have injured your kneecap, you will need a lot more perseverance in life, because you can expect to encounter a few worries.

KNIFE A dream about a knife is never favorable, because it can indicate tears or misunderstandings with people you cherish.

LADDER To climb a ladder and not worry about your climb is excellent, for it indicates greater headway being made by you in achieving your ambitions. Should you be tense and frightened about climbing the ladder, this could indicate some setbacks for you.

LATENESS If you are trying to be punctual in keeping an appointment but for some reason you are late, it means that others around you will be seeking your advice; they think well of you, especially where your ideas are concerned.

LAUNDERING Minor reversals are manifested when you are washing something.

LESSON Being given lessons in any field, and not worrying about them, points to

Dream Interpretations

the expectation of great success in whatever interests you most.

LETTER   A letter, whether you are receiving it or writing it in your dream, foreshadows news that will come to you and could be surprising.

LOAN   To dream that someone is asking you to lend him something indicates that you can expect some losses to come your way.

LOCKS   Not being able to open a door or a case because it is locked, and the inability to find the key, denotes the necessity for more economy. Locking things up, away from someone else, signifies that a secret is being kept from you.

LYING   To tell a lie in your dream is not good, for you could find yourself in some difficult situations with other people. If, on the other hand, you recognize a person who is near to you, and he is telling you a lie, then it denotes just how genuine that person's feelings toward you are and how fond he is of you.

MAGIC   If you dream that happenings are affecting you in almost a magical manner, it indicates that good changes you had thought could not possibly come your way will do so.

Probing the Unknown

MAN   If the man you see is a stranger to you, it is extremely lucky. It is not quite so fortunate for you to dream of meeting a new female companion.

MAP   The consultation of a map indicates you will be making other changes at work, or may be changing your place of abode.

MEAT   To dream that you are attending a dinner and are eating meat is not good, and means that you are slightly overdoing things. If you are preparing a meal yourself, then this is considered to be fairly lucky.

MEDICINE   This is not the luckiest dream to have, especially if you are taking the medicine yourself, but it suggests that you should be able to surmount your problems in time.

MONEY   No matter whether you are receiving or paying out money, this is an extremely good dream. If you find some money, this suggests that something you have been hoping for will happen, but will be slightly delayed. If you win money, it is an indication that more economy is necessary on your part.

MUDDLE   To dream that you are in a muddle and that the more you try to tidy it up the less progress you make is just a small warning that there could be

Dream Interpretations

slight accidents either coming your way or to someone you like.

MUSIC To be able to hear music in your dreams is considered to be extremely lucky, and the more melodic the music, the greater your successes.

NAGGING Nagging, whether you are being nagged or doing the nagging yourself in a dream, is indicative of chatter that can be pleasing or annoying, but really is forewarning you to keep your own confidences.

NAKEDNESS Walking around naked, or even swimming in this state, is considered to be very lucky for you, more so if you are unmarried and in love, because then it denotes great loyalty from the person of your choice, plus a lot of happiness.

NAMES If you hear in your dream that someone is talking about a person who is close to you, and he mentions the name, this could denote a little unhappiness emotionally. If you hear your own name being called, then the indications are that someone is going to ask help from you in the near future.

NECK If you are wearing something around your neck that breaks in your dream, then indications are that your affairs may not be going quite so well in your domestic life for a short while. On the other hand, should someone be admiring your neck, then you are having a love affair that is going to be extremely happy and successful.

NEWS   This is usually a dream of reversal. If the news you hear is good, then you could have to face a slight worry. If it is bad, good luck will follow, but nothing really great.

NOISE   To hear noise in your dream that blocks out all other sounds shows that you yourself may have to be peacemaker with people close to you who are involved in a quarrel.

NOTE   To dream that you are writing a note and trying to get it to someone quickly usually means that you may find yourself having to ask help from someone, but cannot really rely too much on getting it.

NURSE   To see a nurse in your dream is usually a very good sign, because it augurs prosperity where either your work or financial affairs are concerned.

OATH   If you are swearing an oath in your dream, or guaranteeing something, it is almost always a suggestion of good finances for you, and that the outlook for your future is bright.

OATS   Corn or oats or anything of a similar character is considered extremely lucky. In effect, you are guided by knowing that as long as you are doing something, success and happiness will be yours.

OFFER   An offer, good or bad, made to you in your dream is usually a very lucky indication. It denotes that you will be making improvements especially in your working life.

OIL   Oil is not the most fortunate dream to have, because it indicates irritations and frustrations that could delay things around you.

OLD AGE   Your own old age means that you need more confidence and that you have no need for worry, because you should be doing far better than you think in most things you try for.

OPERA   Whether you are sitting and listening to an operatic recording or are indeed at an opera, it is a sign that there could be a few struggles lying ahead with which you must cope.

ORANGE   If the orange you are eating in your dream is sweet and ripe, you can expect good fortune, but if it is tough and rather sharp, then do take care that what you say is not misconstrued by those around you.

OX   To see an ox in your dream is very lucky, but to see more than one ox

Probing the Unknown

	foretells that you should be taking more chances to attain additional goals because this is a period of opportunity for you.
PAIN	This is considered to be an extremely lucky dream. It suggests that you are needed by others, especially those who love you, so that the more pain you experience in your dream, the more happiness and success should come your way.
PAPER	Paper denotes a certain amount of unsettledness. Clean paper means you have a good chance of getting over your difficulties, but soiled or even torn paper indicates it would be better for you to sit on the fence and do nothing for the moment.
PARCEL	Carrying a parcel in your dream, or receiving one, foretells a slight disappointment for you. On the other hand, receiving a big parcel points at changes for you and is not considered unlucky.
PEN	To dream that you can see someone writing a letter with a pen, or even that you yourself are using a pen, portends that you will be receiving news from a person you have not heard of for some time.
PERFUME	This is a propitious dream even if you are not using the perfume yourself.

Dream Interpretations

For an eligible person who is beginning an affair, this is always an indication that the affair is fortunate and will go very well.

PILL — A bottle of pills, or the action of taking pills, indicates travel that you should enjoy.

PISTOL — If you are handling or firing a pistol in your dream, take this as a warning that you should be looking for a change in your life, because even after much hard work you will make very little headway in what you are now doing.

POLICE — Talking to a policeman or dealing with the police in some particular case denotes help that should be coming to you regarding a problem you have, and this help should enable you to overcome your difficulties.

QUARREL — To dream that you are quarreling with someone often denotes jealousy, but can also indicate that you will meet success and good luck in your working or financial field.

QUEEN — Royalty in a dream augurs well, because it indicates not only help from those around, but great luck.

QUESTIONS — If you are either asking questions or being asked questions in your dream, this suggests you have a few difficulties that you must try to overcome, but that patience should enable you to do this.

QUILT The more luxurious your quilt, or the more colorful your quilt, the greater should be your good fortune.

RAIN If the rain you see in the dream is only a drizzle, you must have patience with a few frustrations in life. If you are walking through a very heavy downpour, then you had better fortify yourself against something that is depressing.

RAT This is not a good omen because it suggests dishonesty and deception from someone you know. If you are being protected from a rat in your dream and you recognize the person who is shielding you, it indicates that person is extremely genuine toward you.

RECONCIL- To be reconciled with someone with
IATION whom you have quarreled is a lucky dream for you.

RELIGION This is not considered to be fortunate if you are worried about a religious problem in the dream. But if you are calm and happy, this is an excellent sign, because it connotes peace of mind.

Dream Interpretations

REVENGE — This is a dream that can indicate a quarrel brought about by your own obstinacy, and you have been just as much to blame as the person with whom you are quarreling.

RIBBONS — While this is quite a fortunate dream, at the same time it indicates you will be spending more than you can afford.

RIVER — If you see a river that looks turbulent because the weather is not good, you can prepare yourself for slight upsets in your ambitions. If, on the other hand, the sun is out and the river you see is clear, this foretells a journey.

ROSES — A very propitious dream, and more so if your roses are in full bloom. It denotes luck in most directions, especially where your love life is concerned.

SALT — Salt foretells that your finances are going to be stable. There is an old saying, "The more salt you keep in your house, the more good money and good health will come your way."

SCISSORS — A pair of scissors is a forewarning of someone being disloyal to you. If you recognize the person in your dream who is using the scissors, then you would be well advised not to let him know too much.

SHIP — To be aboard a ship making for the

harbor, or to be able to see the shore, is fortunate because it suggests things are going to go very well for you.

SHOP   To dream that you own a shop or are working in that shop denotes that your affairs are muddled; on the other hand, if you are extremely busy in this shop, then you will know that the muddle will eventually be cleared up.

SIGH   A dream that you are sighing fortunately has the reverse meaning, that you are due for a great deal of happiness and laughter.

SILK   This is an unfortunate dream, especially for a woman, because it points to dishonesty around her. If a man dreams of silk, it indicates luck where his business is concerned.

SMOKING   Smoking invariably indicates disappointments and frustrations for you. *See also* CIGARETTE.

SWIMMING   If you have difficulty swimming in your dream, it is usually thought that a little treachery is going on around you, but if you are happily swimming, then without a doubt success should be yours.

TAP   A water tap that is running clearly and regularly is an extremely good signpost that many affairs are going to be trouble-free for you.

Dream Interpretations

TAXI Inability to find a taxi in your dream and annoyance about this usually denote that someone is telling you lies. On the other hand, should you get your taxi easily and progress toward your destination without difficulty, a very pleasing letter is on its way to you.

TEA Drinking tea and enjoying it suggest that you are not persevering enough in order to achieve your ends.

TEETH This is not a good dream because it indicates that your health may not be absolutely up to par.

THROAT If your throat is uncomfortable and causing you slight trouble in your dreams, it is considered to be quite lucky, and therefore the sooner you can clear your throat the quicker will be your success.

TIN To see smooth tin in your dream indicates that you have deceit around you and you will surmount it, but jagged tin signifies you have a few false friends.

TIREDNESS If you feel very tired in your dream and are aware of it, this means almost what it says, because you could lose ground by not taking sufficient rest.

TOYS Toys in a dream usually portend that a member of your family is going to

Probing the Unknown

	take a test or an examination and will be successful.
TRUCK	Dreaming that you are either driving a truck or are just seeing a truck is certainly not the best of dreams. It warns you that you are being too impatient about things. At the same time, it advises you that more patience and perseverance will make things eventually turn out the way you want.
UGLINESS	To dream that you yourself are ugly or that you are talking to someone who is ugly denotes great good fortune for you.
UMBRELLA	An open umbrella in your dream is lucky, because in effect it denotes that you are coming out of rain and cloud into sunshine.
UNDRESSING	Undressing or being undressed in front of other people usually is a sign that chatter or scandal will make you unhappy, but dreaming that you are naked is fortunate.
UNHAPPINESS	To be unhappy in a dream merely shows that you are being very wise, cautious, and patient in your life, and that good luck should be with you because of this.
UNIFORM	To dream that you see yourself wearing a uniform or recognize a person who is wearing a uniform suggests

Dream Interpretations

not only that this person thinks very highly of you, but that peace of mind and happiness in your domestic life will be yours.

UNKINDNESS To dream that someone is unkind to you and not considerate of you, or that you yourself are unkind to a person familiar to you, really indicates how loyal and genuine that person, or the person of your choice, is toward you.

VASE A vase is a warning that you should be more thoughtful of other people and that you are being too vain and egotistical.

VEXATION If you find yourself very vexed with someone around you in your dream, this foretells good headway for you, plus pleasing fortunes.

VICTORY You reverse this dream of victory; it indicates that you should not get involved in arguments or take other people's sides where their personal quarrels are concerned.

VINE As long as the vine in your dream is full of fruit, then success is about to come your way after hard work. On the other hand, should you be working hard and the fruit is not to be seen on the vine, it points to the fact that you need to make certain changes in your life.

Probing the Unknown

VIOLIN — To hear a beautiful melody being played on a violin indicates that you are going to be very popular with most people. On the other hand, if one of the strings of the violin breaks in the dream, then you yourself will have to be the peacemaker in patching up a quarrel between two other people.

VOICES — A lot of people chattering is not a good dream because it denotes that there could be holdups and frustrations ahead for you in most things.

WAGES — When you dream that you are either receiving wages or paying out wages, it is not favorable and suggests there is someone around you who is not honest.

WALKING — Irritations are indicated, but if you are striding in a determined manner, it shows that you will get over these irritations with time.

WAR — This unfortunate dream warns of slight dangers ahead for you.

WEB — To dream that you are either spinning a web or are in a web is good, because it indicates you should attain most of your ambitions.

WIG — If you see a wig in your dream, it points to indecision regarding your

Dream Interpretations

choice between two people in your love life.

WINE — Wine, in any circumstance, denotes a very happy domestic period for you.

WITCH — A witch is not lucky and warns you to take special precautions, for the moment, in all circumstances.

YARN — Handling yarn or spinning yarn tells you that either good news or an unexpected gift should be coming to you in the near future.

YAWN — If you dream that you cannot stop yawning, this denotes that you are not giving enough attention to the small details and could be sorry if you do not concentrate more on them.

YELLOW — To dream of the color yellow indicates that there is jealousy around you.

YOLK — The yolk of an egg is a lucky sign, especially if you are a gambler, for it indicates winnings. If you are not a gambler, then this just foretells good fortune.

ZIPPER — If the zipper on your dress or trousers is working freely, then you can expect good news to come quickly. However, should your zipper stick or be difficult to handle, then you may expect to en-

Probing the Unknown

counter some obstacles that will have to be surmounted.

ZIRCON As you know, a zircon is a brownish gem, and a dream involving one is not considered fortunate. It foretells of deceit around you and postponements where your plans are concerned.

ZODIAC If you are attempting to study the characteristics of the sign of the zodiac in your dream, or even just one sign, then this means that you are going to prosper greatly by concentrating and learning.

ZOO As long as you are not being attacked by an animal in your visit to a zoo, then this dream is considered to be extremely lucky.

4.

Responsibilities of Being a Psychic

Quite often I am asked, "What is the use of such guessing of the future, when it is admittedly not surely known?"

Many people are of this opinion, but I don't think one can make such a statement. I would like to make it very clear here and now that the true psychic does not make guesses; he or she possesses the gift of extrasensory perception. What he predicts at a certain moment of time may make no sense to the sitter, or might even appear ridiculous, but in many cases will turn out to be correct—not necessarily to the absolute date or time that is mentioned. As I have often said, most psychics have a time differential—which in other words means that they can be from a period of one to ten. I can only speak from my own experience, of course, and I have been praised by the world's press and private clients as being either bang on time when I said a certain thing would happen or a

Probing the Unknown

"one out," which could mean one week, one month, or even one year. I will give you an example of this:

In 1958 I was asked to give a reading to a very pretty young lady in London who was a stenographer by profession. In my reading I told her that she was in love with a gentleman who was not English—he was tall, had blue eyes, wore an army uniform, and was of high rank. I told her at that time that she could not marry him, even though he was genuinely in love with her, because he was already married and had no real complaint against his wife, other than the fact that they had fallen out of love and were married in name only.

I told her that by July 24 of that year this gentleman's wife would divorce him, and this in turn would make him quite angry, because, like most men, he would like to have been in the position of being the person to sue for divorce.

I well remember saying to her, "But who cares who makes the break that is wanted, just as long as it is made with not too much unhappiness?"

I then went on to tell her that she would cross the water to a fairly warm climate, and the place she would live in would have a capital *c* in its name, and it would be here that she would marry this gentleman, but that she had better enjoy the two years of her marriage because her husband would be a great deal older than herself and would have a bad leg and would die.

July 24 came and went, and suddenly I received a telephone call from this young girl, who said, "So much for your prediction about my marrying this American general by July 24."

A year later I had to go to Gibraltar to do some television shows and decided I would stay in Tangier, Morocco, which was only a fifteen-minute hop by plane

Responsibilities of Being a Psychic

from Gibraltar. When I arrived at my hotel in Tangier, reporters were there to interview me and the newspapers appeared the following morning with quite a spread.

Three days later I received a letter from Casablanca from this young lady, saying she had read in the papers that I was in Tangier and would like to apologize for being so rude to me on the telephone, but that she had married the general, as I had predicted, on July 24—only exactly one year later than I had prophesied. Much later she again wrote to me in England to say that she had had two of the happiest years of her life, but had unfortunately lost her husband because he had developed gangrene of the leg and died. This explains the time differential.

I consider myself lucky to be only a "one out" when wrong but, as I have said, you can have extremely genuine clairvoyants who can be up to a "ten out," and I personally would never say they were making stupid guesses about the future, or were completely wrong, because I have seen so much proof in my lifetime of how many times they are right as opposed to wrong.

I well remember a reader sending me a little card on which was plainly printed, "When you are right, no one remembers; when you are wrong, no one forgets," and this is so true of life.

Many clients come to me and want me really to confirm what is in their mind, and these are sincere individuals with good common sense. When I do not confirm what they wish to hear—and this happens quite a lot—then they become annoyed.

Another view that is often stated, and really angers me, is that well-known clairvoyants can sway the thinking powers of their clients and dominate their reactions. I have even heard it said that clairvoyants can influence the morals of a client. This is absolute rubbish. You must remember that all human beings have free will, and only those who wanted to be swayed in one direction or the other would fall for such hokum. A hypnotist cannot make his sitter commit an immoral or illegal act when under hypnosis that he would not do of his own free will; the same situation applies to the predictors in this world.

Kim Novak, who is a very good friend of mine as well as a client, came to me in London a few years ago for a reading. I told her there was a tall, dark gentleman around her with brown or hazel eyes, who had the initial R, and that he would be very good for her and she would marry him.

Kim is one of the most natural people it has been my joy to meet, because she bubbles over with gaiety and yet at the same time has great depths of good common sense. When I told her this she seemed highly delighted. However, a little confusion ensued, because at the time Kim was seeing a lot of that very well-known columnist, Roderick Mann, who is the Earl Wilson or Leonard Lyons of England. A short while after Kim had seen me, everybody began to think she would marry Roderick but, in fact, within a very short space of time she married the English film star, Richard Johnston. I did not get anything other than the fact that her future husband would be a tallish man with dark complexion and brown eyes, which both Roderick Mann and Richard Johnston had.

I would now like to make another prediction for Kim, which will not be a guess. In my opinion, Kim will marry again, and again the man's initial will be R, and this marriage will be happy. Within the next few months we shall also see a small collection of paintings on exhibition done by Kim.

Another example of how a person can be out in time,

Responsibilities of Being a Psychic

in my instance, was with that famous television personality, Virginia Graham, who will be remembered for her very successful, long-running series, "Girl Talk." While my show, "Maurice Woodruff Predicts," was running on television in the United States in 1969, I invited Virginia to appear as one of my guests. She had just finished "Girl Talk," and I found her to be a lovable, voluble, enchanting character who was absolutely made for television and public appearances, for she possesses a quick wit and a magnetic personality.

I predicted for Virginia that she would be offered a new and better series that would become even bigger than "Girl Talk" had been for her. This did not happen within the year 1969, but in March, 1970, I am delighted to say that Virginia was offered this new series. At the time of writing this book, the show as such has not yet started, but is due to commence in the near future. Here again, while I was not right in my absolute timing, my prediction did come off in the period of a "one" later—in other words, a year. And I will say here and now that this show of Virginia Graham's will be an enormous success.

The ability to forecast the future has been bestowed on many men and women throughout the ages. One such man, extraordinarily gifted in the occult, was Nostradamus.

When the Romans drove their enemies out of Jerusalem, these refugees fled to all parts of the world. It has been said that most of them took flight into Provence and settled there, and were treated quite well. They became masters in their own fields and earned fairly good livings as notaries, physicians, merchants of materials, and artists.

History records that King René invited two of them to become his physicians, and one of these physicians was

Probing the Unknown

named Pierre de Nostre-Dame. He was not only a doctor of medicine, but also had a great knowledge of astrology and the occult.

One of his relatives had a son named Michel de Nostradamus who was born in 1503. In later years he became world famous for his extraordinary predictions. In addition, he established quite a reputation as a healer. When the black plague descended upon Europe, Nostradamus found himself not agreeing with the celebrated physicians and professors of that day who believed that the only way to overcome the plague was by fumigating. He also believed that an analysis should be made of the victim's excreta, but he was shouted down, and so for quite a few years he wandered from place to place, especially in Bordeaux and Avignon, treating victims of the plague in his own way. Many of those afflicted with the plague recovered under his ministrations, and it has been said that he was, in fact, the instigator of antiseptic medicine.

While many doctors of the day contracted the plague, Nostradamus appears to have been lucky, because his health remained sturdy. When the plague had finally run its course, Nostradamus was highly honored. He was looked upon almost as a miracle worker, or saint. He married and had two sons, but actually outlived his wife and children. For some time after their deaths Nostradamus retired to a monastery and reverently followed the monastery's rulings. A short while later the plague broke out again in the south of France, and he was asked to go and help save an area literally gutted by this terrible disease.

Nostradamus was successful in his endeavor to control the plague. Consequently he was voted a pension for life and given many gifts of money and jewels. He married

Responsibilities of Being a Psychic

for a second time and settled down finally in Provence, where people came from all over to consult him. Doctors branded him with the name of sorcerer, and there may have been a slight truth in this accusation because he used many strange instruments, such as a divining wand and magic mirrors. His biographer, Geane Aymes de Chavigny, related one of Nostradamus's own explanations regarding his actions. He was inspired by the prophetic spirit, he said, this being the gift of providence, which can only be interpreted as a sixth sense, the gift to foresee. He was a wonderful astrologer, even if his methods were different from others of his day.

Everyone who has at any time written about this fantastic man agrees that Nostradamus was many years ahead of his time and possessed supernormal knowledge. At least one hundred years before Isaac Newton's law of gravitation, Nostradamus had foreseen it. There is little doubt that he was regarded as the greatest prophet of his day. He recorded his visions almost under a hypnotic spell similar to that of Edgar Cayce, America's greatest mystic, and there is one thing he stated that can never be disputed: "After my earthly passing, my writ will do more than during life." There have indeed been many books published about this brilliant prophet.

In fifteenth-century England, Old Mother Shipton, who was regarded in her day as a witch, wrote her predictions in the form of poetry. There is little doubt that her predictions were extremely accurate. She forecast that ships would go under the sea, that man would chew a substance and smoke it, that man would eat a solid round object taken out of the earth, and that men would fly like birds in the sky. Of course we all know these predictions involve the submarine, the chewing and smoking of

Probing the Unknown

tobacco, the eating of potatoes, and airplanes. Although not a doctor, Mother Shipton apparently became well known for her herbal treatments.

The remarkable Leonardo da Vinci was able to visualize such things as an X-rayed hand hundreds of years before the X ray was ever thought of, let alone used; this hand proved to be perfect in every detail. He even developed the concept for the famous Bailey bridges, which were not used until World War II. These bridges could be constructed rapidly and greatly aided the invasion forces. Da Vinci was, of course, a great scholar and, as the world knows, a wonderful painter.

In our own times there was the famous British author, H. G. Wells, who wrote many futuristic works, including his famous *The Shape of Things to Come*, in which he sent men flying into space.

I can recall my own mother, Vera Woodruff, telling friends one evening at dinner, long before World War II broke out, that within the space of a few years people would be living underground for a period because they would be terrified of what was going on above. She was foreseeing the war and people fleeing underground to the bomb shelters.

Most of us must have read in the newspapers of Jeane Dixon's forecasts, and only recently at a party I met a man who told me he had consulted Mrs. Dixon when he was in Washington. She had shocked him completely by telling him things that even his closest friends did not know.

Here are six people who were, in their vision capabilities, years ahead of their day, and were gifted with very strong clairvoyance or extrasensory perception.

Many of the deep thinkers of the world ask, "How is

Responsibilities of Being a Psychic

it that astrology and clairvoyance did not help the great civilizations of the past, good and bad, so that they could see and survive?"

My answer to this question is that quite a few people will consult an astrologer or a clairvoyant merely to have their own ideas confirmed. They are really not concerned about learning the truth. I myself will not confirm a person's ideas unless through my work I see that affairs will turn out that way. I would rather offend the person by being honest, for at least then my conscience and my belief in my work will not be harmed.

You must also consider the leadership of such a country as Nazi Germany. Adolf Hitler believed in both clairvoyance and astrology, and had his own personal clairvoyant. At the same time, he was so adamant in his convictions about conquering the Jews, Poland, and Western Europe that he would not accept the truth from his clairvoyant. It is also fairly obvious that because of Hitler's obsession with power, his clairvoyant must have been afraid to tell him the whole truth and felt it better to inform him only about the good things, not the bad.

Can you imagine such people as Emperor Nero of Rome or King Herod of Judea accepting defeatist predictions? Of course they would not. These leaders were so full of their own ambitions that, to their way of thinking, the world was made for them, and the desires and beliefs created in their warped minds were exactly how things should turn out. The seers in these particular instances had little alternative but to corroborate the belief that affairs would be as the leaders wished. The late Robert Naylor, the English astrologer who created the phrase, "What the stars foretell," was asked by a certain newspaper if he would say that World War II was going to end quickly. He refused to say so because his work told him otherwise, and he is the only person I have known to have the courage to stand by his working beliefs. He only divulged the information that the charts told him was certain.

Basically, no matter what predictions one makes, whether by clairvoyance or astrology, the result becomes "destiny." Throughout history this word has been given a wrong definition, since some folk mention it with a feeling of reproach, while others do not believe in it at all.

Some people say, "Well, if it is in my destiny that this will happen, then it will happen anyhow, regardless of whether I consult an astrologer or a clairvoyant."

This is not really true, for, as I have said, my work falls more into the lines of guidance, not necessarily absolute destiny. Surely the only things that are predestined are birth and death, so that everything that occurs between these two points invariably has a two-way direction. It is my job when looking into the future to state that a certain thing is going to happen, but that it can happen in one way or another; if you would like my advice, you would of course approach it in the way I recommend because my work tells me that this would be the easier direction for you to take. When making a statement, any clairvoyant who is worth his salt will not just say to a person that he is going to move; the clairvoyant will explain why the person is going to move, if possible where he is going to move, and what the result of that move will be.

I will admit, quite frankly, that in the occult field throughout the years there have been a lot of charlatans. It is these people who have done our science untold harm, because they live on the trust of those who come to consult them and they deserve to be condemned. The old and true saying, "The proof of the pudding is in the eat-

Responsibilities of Being a Psychic

ing," applies to any client who is fortunate enough to have a genuine clairvoyant or astrologer who has proved over the years to be accurate and honest. He should stick to that psychic and not get confused by consulting with all and sundry. Every one of us strives for knowledge and self-understanding in order to better cope with the increased anxiety and insecurity that are factors in our daily lives.

I do have an excuse for the psychics of the past who dishonestly advised leaders of great countries that went adrift. In order to foretell events, one must have sympathy for one's fellow being and know what makes that person tick. We all have human frailties and, since these futurecasters knew the strength and ambition of people such as Adolf Hitler, they took shortcuts to please those leaders. This was the betrayal of their psychic powers.

As I have always said, "No one is infallible."

When I hear such people as Peter Sellers or England's Lady Boyle state, "I never make my mind up about anything of great importance before I consult Maurice Woodruff" or "I go to Maurice Woodruff as one might go to one's doctor or adviser," it concerns me because I would hate to have to shoulder the responsibilities of so influencing a person's every move. My function is to guide my client.

An illustration of my point about the responsibility of making a prediction come true involves the actor, Richard Harris. He came to see me in London and I gave him this reading: The next part he played would be either a sailor or a seafaring man. I also predicted his divorce, which has since occurred. I found Richard to be a man who knew his own mind completely, but also a very gentle and very sweet man. I would say here that he has been exceptionally

Probing the Unknown

kind throughout his life, but quite naturally has met with problems from time to time and has resented this.

As it turned out, the very next part Richard was offered was in fact that of a sailor, but when he started shooting the film he found that he did not like the role. He could not be in sympathy with it, and he voluntarily gave it up. In other words, he used his own free will and did not try to make my prediction come true.

Many years ago I met a very beautiful lady in London and I was informed only of her first name, Hazel. I gave her a reading at a charity bazaar and said that she would marry a man who made a lot of money by building, that she would be of tremendous help to him, and that he would become immensely wealthy. Hazel, who had a terrific sense of humor, boomed out with laughter and said, "Well, if that is true, Mr. Woodruff, I shall certainly let you know!"

I did not see Hazel again for a period of some six or seven years, until I attended a party given by friends of mine who lived in a beautiful house at Sunningdale, England, very near to the famous Ascot racecourse. Hazel came rushing across the room to me and said, "Maurice, how good to see you. You may remember that you said I would marry a man who did some building. Well, I am now Mrs. Ronald Lyons." Ronald Lyons is one of England's biggest builders. Not only has he built housing estates, but also London Airport and apartment blocks in Majorca, Spain. They have a yacht, they bought the Duke of Windsor's house next to Ascot, and they have their own private box at Ascot, to which I have been invited on several occasions.

Hazel could not have made her prediction come true, because she did not know her husband at the time I gave her the reading. She told me later that after Ronald had proposed to her, and she had accepted, she was going through an old handbag one day. She came across the notes she had made on my predictions and she said to a friend who was with her, "My God! That clairvoyant Maurice Woodruff was right. He said that I would marry a man who made money by building, and that man would have an R or L for one of his initials!"

It is my opinion that when one goes to a clairvoyant, or anyone in similar work, for a consultation, he never should go with the intention of believing every single thing that clairvoyant tells him. It is unfair to the clairvoyant and to the person consulting him, since this could cause the client to lose out in the long run. The clairvoyant's very awareness that his or her sitter is going to devour and believe every single prediction made during the consultation must, at times, stop that medium from saying things that he normally would say.

It is the major issues that are the important ones, and if you have ever had a reading, then you know that there are a lot of major issues. But there are also quite a few minor ones, and it is on the minor issues that the clairvoyant can be either completely out or delayed in time. I know of clairvoyants who have clients referred to them by other members of their profession simply because the client had become too heavy a responsibility. Very luckily I have never had to do this, but I have had such people sent on to me.

In 1965 I had a rather unhappy experience. I was in Hollywood and a very good friend, Richard Gully, telephoned me to say that an extremely wealthy gentleman whose name was Arthur Cameron would like to give a dinner at the Beverly Hilton Hotel with me as guest of honor. He asked if the following Wednesday night would suit me.

Probing the Unknown

I said, "Well, yes, Richard, I would love to come and feel highly honored that Mr. Cameron wishes to give the party for me, but I am rather worried about his health."

Richard replied, "No, Maurice, Mr. Cameron was ill about four years ago, but he is perfectly well now." He added, "There are going to be some very interesting people at the dinner."

When the day in question arrived, I received a phone call from Richard to say that, since Mr. Cameron was not feeling very well, Dorothy Malone was going to be the hostess at the dinner party during his absence that night. I arrived at the dinner and had a jolly evening with such good and dear friends as Glenn Ford, Richard Harris, and Dorothy Malone.

The next morning Richard Gully phoned me and said, "Maurice, your concern for Arthur Cameron's health was well founded. Arthur Cameron died during the night!"

This is the type of prediction that at all times makes me unhappy. I had not told Richard all I knew about this gentleman's health. Although I had never met him, I somehow knew deep within me that he would die.

It was also in this same year, while in Hollywood, that I met Ann Miller, who has since become a very good friend of mine. I gave her a reading, and I said that her mother would be coming out of a bank in Beverly Hills and would have a fall down two or three steps and would be rushed to the hospital. I told Ann not to worry, because even though it might seem that she had injured herself badly, she would be all right.

Several weeks later, as I was having dinner, the telephone rang. Ann Miller called to tell me, "Maurice, you were so right. My mother was coming out of the bank today in Beverly Hills and she missed her footing and fell down the stairs, and they rushed her to the hospital.

Responsibilities of Being a Psychic

I was rehearsing for a television special and they called me at the studio. I rushed to the hospital, where they told me that they were going to x-ray my mother because they thought she may have broken either one or both of her legs. I quite calmly told them that they need not bother to x-ray her, because I knew she would be all right, and that all she would be suffering from was shock. They insisted on going ahead with the X rays, and afterward they told me that my mother was in no way injured, other than just a little shock, but how on earth did I know that there was no need for X rays?

"My answer to them was, 'Maurice Woodruff told me about this several weeks ago!'"

I certainly feel that I took on a responsibility in telling Ann this.

I mentioned earlier that I was famous for being only a "one out" in time when making predictions, but I have also been known to be wrong, inasmuch as, on rare occasions, that which I have said may not have come to pass. Fortunately, my average of success to date has been far, far greater than my average of failure. I believe quite sincerely that the only reason for this is because, when I am talking to a client, unless a thing is absolutely firmly set in my mind, I will not state it. I could, of course, be right, but the fact that I have a doubt makes me inclined not to mention it at all.

Another point I would like to make clear is that any clairvoyant who allows his, or her, personal feelings or sympathy for the sitter to come into the picture is bound to be more wrong than right. When giving a reading, whether it be to a private client or a member of the audience of a stage or television show, the clairvoyant must remain completely neutral in his thoughts and feelings.

Probing the Unknown

I well remember making a very bad mistake a few years ago in England. There was a general election to be decided between the Conservatives, headed by Edward Heath, and the Socialists, headed by then Prime Minister Harold Wilson. At the time I was asked to appear as celebrity guest at London's Palladium Theatre, where a spectacular called "Sunday Night at the Palladium" was being televised. Until this time all celebrity guests who were appearing at the show merely had to stand up in their seats when their names were announced from the stage and acknowledge the audience's applause. You can imagine my surprise when I stood up and found that I had a microphone thrust into my hand. I was not prepared to make predictions, but I said that within two or three weeks one artist in the show, Matt Munroe, would acquire a new Rolls-Royce automobile. At the same time I said that the Conservatives would win the general election.

The first prediction came true, as Matt telephoned me in three weeks and informed me that he had been given a beautiful new Rolls-Royce. But the second prediction was absolutely wrong, and I knew why. My sympathies were much, much more with the Conservative party than with the Socialists, and I wanted them to win the election, which was not only wrong but extremely mischievous of me.

The mistakes a clairvoyant makes might more properly be called "mix-ups," because quite often when giving a reading he or she will get his facts absolutely right but the sitter may have many intimate friends and the predictions may alight on the wrong person.

I always wish to be known as a human being, and the day that I do not make a mistake, however rare, will be the day that I shall want to give up this work.

5.
Reminiscences

Over the years I have found that most people have a really strong urge to find relief from the tension of uncertainty by being informed of what is in their future.

I was very especially pleased and honored in 1956 when I was asked by my very good friend Major Donald Neville-Willing to work in London's famous Café de Paris, which was at that time one of the most glamorous night spots in the whole of Europe.

Looking back at this period, I realize now how fortunate I was to be performing at the café in its heyday, because one could see some unforgettable performances from stars of the caliber of Carl Brisson, Tallulah Bankhead, Noel Coward, Hermione Gingold, Marlene Dietrich, and Eartha Kitt. I was in a position to be able to advise quite a few of them, as well as the hundreds of society

Probing the Unknown

and show business folk who came to my private table on the balcony.

I predicted to Hermione Gingold that she would visit America and would enjoy fabulous success, which has certainly turned out to be the case.

I told Sophie Tucker that she would write a best seller —as her autobiography later proved to be.

Although I cannot apply my clairvoyant gift to myself, I have always had strong premonitions of the crises in my life. Early on the afternoon of April 23, 1957, I was sitting quietly, resting in the lounge of my house between clients, when I heard an ominous sound; the room seemed instantly to fill with the traffic noise of the street outside.

In the past, when things were not going to go well for me, I had had this same experience, and it used to worry me. While I was wondering what kind of trouble this could mean, a large cushion on a chair at the other side of the fireplace dropped with quite a thud to the floor. Glancing at the clock, I noticed it was 2:30 P.M.

I was too busy the rest of the day to brood over this premonition. I spent the evening at the Café de Paris in my usual style, and shortly before midnight had dinner with my business manager of those days—Bill Thomas. As midnight struck there was the usual drum roll from the orchestra, the soft lights switched to the top of the famous staircase down which so many stars have made their entrances, and there stood Sophie Tucker.

Bill Thomas grabbed my arm. "Good heavens, Maurice —it's your mother!"

For a second, as I looked at Sophie, I could have sworn it was my mother standing there. Very early next morning I received a call from the hospital where my mother had been a patient for some weeks. They had only just found out my whereabouts.

Reminiscences

My mother had died at 2:30 P.M. *the previous afternoon*, April 23, 1957.

It seemed to me that every time I met Sophie Tucker something bad happened for me, although we were always the very best of friends. In 1963, my English lawyer, David Jacobs, who was very well known to many American stars, decided to give a big party at his seaside home, near Brighton, in England. Both Bill Thomas and I were invited. David made Sophie Tucker his guest of honor for the occasion, and of course Sophie and I met, laughed, and chattered together once again. That very same night—in fact, within a half hour of leaving the party—on returning to our hotel, Bill collapsed and died. You can well imagine how nervous I then became about the prospect of meeting Sophie again.

However, the point of this story concerns David Jacobs, who entertained Sophie Tucker a great deal during her lifetime. David was not only a brilliant solicitor, but a truly wonderful man; he died quite tragically in 1968. Later, when I read in the papers of Sophie's death while I was in the south of France, I found myself feeling greatly relieved, although it sounds like quite a wicked thing to say. I had been talking with friends about Sophie a week before her death, after which my new manager, Harry Arnold, who is still with me, was taken quite sick; very luckily he got better.

My mother, who was regarded as the greatest clairvoyant of the thirties, never hesitated at any time to tell people that they were near death. But I have always felt strongly that unless my insight can definitely help the person involved, by perhaps enabling him to make a will or change a will, it would be callous to reveal the inevitable and would worry him unnecessarily. I may, however, tell a relative if I estimate it would be helpful.

Probing the Unknown

I was first trained to be a tailor in London's famous Savile Row, where I returned to work after World War II. But I knew for certain that my career lay in clairvoyancy and, like most beginners in any profession, I badly needed a lucky break. It was to come quite unexpectedly.

My mother telephoned me one day in 1946 and asked me if I would stand in for her during a week at a charity bazaar in aid of the British Red Cross. There would be no pay, but it meant I would have an opportunity to give readings to people who might later become my clients.

In those days my salary at tailoring was fifteen dollars a week, but I spent three dollars on having a hundred visiting cards printed, pressed my suit myself, and took a bus to Westminster.

For five hours I sat in a rather stuffy booth and forecast the future for fifty people. Each of these people had to pay a dollar to the charity, and quite a few of them left with one of my visiting cards. Just as I had hoped, the requests for appointments began to come in for me, but I can assure you that first year on my own was really hard going. I charged a $1.50 fee for a reading, and it was a good week when I made enough to cover my expenses.

I have always said that no matter how bad things may be for you at certain periods in life, compensations do follow. And so it was for me. I found that I had got myself into debt and was compelled to take a part-time job. Since I had always been interested in interior decorating, I turned to making lampshades in lace and satin. Then I suddenly found that there was a rush of clients for readings, and I was spending two or three evenings a week working at charity balls and giving my services free as well.

It was at one of these charities in London's famous

Reminiscences

Dorchester Hotel that I first met Antony Armstrong-Jones, now, of course, Lord Snowdon. At that time he was an unknown, quite ambitious young photographer, and for him, as for me, the round of charity functions was a means of getting his work known. At this particular affair —the Golden Cage Ball—Tony had borrowed an idea from the seaside "while-you-wait" cameraman; he was raking in the money for charity by photographing giggling debutantes and their escorts with their heads stuck through the hole in the comic backcloth.

Toward the end of that evening, when the rush had slackened off, we stood together and watched the dancing. "What do you see in my future?" he asked.

"That's easy," I said. "Before long you will find yourself working for a man with the initial N in his name, and from then on you will go from success to success."

Tony later joined Baron Nahum (the Baron was the photographer by appointment to the Queen), and the future Lord Snowdon soon began to make a very big reputation in his own right.

One day I discovered that my secretary had filled in a date in my diary with a name that was unfamiliar to me —a Miss Robinson. When she arrived, she turned out to be a charming girl with a soft American accent.

"You will have to warn your father to take great care of his eyes," I told her. "Otherwise he may have a bad accident. You are going to change your work, and I think you will go into television or radio. There are two men in your life, one American and the other English. You won't marry either of them, but the man you do marry will be American." Just then there was a ring at my front door. A young man standing outside asked, "Is Miss Sharman Douglas here?"

As soon as I realized who my client was, I knew that in

143

Probing the Unknown

telling her of her father I had seen the past. The previous week, the then United States ambassador, Lewis Douglas, had badly injured an eye with a hook while out fly-fishing.

As for Sharman, she returned to America at that period to work in television, and she eventually did marry an American.

I sensed tragedy the moment the lovely English starlet, Simone Silva, came into my consulting room and asked me if I could give her some guidance on her future.

"You are planning to cross the water," I said, "and this journey you are going to take has something to do with films. Do not go! I foresee a very unpleasant incident which, in turn, can only lead to bad publicity for you."

Simone, who was a beautiful girl, with a truly wonderful nature, looked distressed. "But, Maurice, I am flying to the Cannes Film Festival in three days' time. I have got to go," she said. "It's terribly important to my career."

I urged her to cancel the flight. "Frankly, Simone, you will have to tread very, very carefully, or else you will be in for a run of trouble—and I must warn you that it is linked with two men, both with the initial B in their names."

Ignoring my advice, Simone flew to Cannes, but was asked to leave by a scandalized festival committee after she was photographed on the beach wearing only the lower half of a bikini. With Simone at the time was Bob Mitchum. Later, when Simone's husband sued for divorce, actor Bonar Colleano was cited in the suit.

Simone came to see me again and admitted that I had been right. Unfortunately, once again I had an overpowering feeling of tragedy in store for this very vital, talented girl. She told me that she was going to Hollywood and wanted to know if she would get a contract. I assured her that she would but I added, "You will not do a single day's filming." I just did not have the heart to tell her all that I saw in her eyes.

When Simone arrived in Hollywood, the Cannes affair followed her. Unfortunately, she never made a film in Hollywood, even though she was given a contract. The late Hedda Hopper and Louella Parsons had heard the Cannes story, and of course printed it for all to know.

Heartbroken, she returned home to England and in November, 1957, shortly before she was due to open in a Mayfair cabaret, she was found dead in her bedroom.

Should I have told her all her fate? I may be wrong, but I still think that I was right in not doing so.

I do not claim that my gift of clairvoyance is unique. In actual fact, I quite sincerely believe, as I have said on both television and radio, that most intelligent people are psychic. Yet even the very few who realize they have this power seldom try to develop it—or they are afraid of what they regard as their premonitions: a woman's "intuition"; the twin sister who has a sudden feeling that her twin who is miles away needs her desperately; the mother who knows instinctively when her child is in danger; that strange "I have been here before" feeling.

We all know that these are familiar examples of latent psychic power at work. Now, if you are really psychic, you will find that mental pictures come into your mind as you look into someone's eyes. They will not come as blurred dreams but as crystal clear images complete in almost every detail. I have found from experience that I can see, for example, not only the location of a house or building—whether it is on a corner, or even in the middle of a row of houses—but straight through it and into almost every room. It is obvious the eyes act as an extremely

Probing the Unknown

powerful focal point. The truly psychic person can "see" things no matter where or what situation he or she is in, and I know that "looking into the future" fascinates everyone, from cabinet ministers to the man paying four or five dollars to have his palm read by a palmist or a swarthy gypsy on a seaside boardwalk.

Quite a surprising number of hardheaded businessmen come to consult me about their problems. Others come to consult me as a kind of regular checkup, much as you and I would go to the doctor or dentist. A while ago I told a property tycoon, "I can see a very large building involving a great deal of money, and I sense a lot of worry hanging over the building." The property man admitted he was considering buying an office block for nearly $3 million, but was unable to make up his mind about this. I advised him that he should buy it. He did so, and eventually made a very large profit on his investment.

All my working life, when making predictions I have tried not to protect myself or my reputation by talking in vague generalities. I happen to believe sincerely in my gift, so I believe in sticking my neck out. In the past ten years I have spent quite a lot of my time in Hollywood, and I do advise many of the film capital's top stars.

When I first arrived in Los Angeles at the invitation of Stephen Boyd in June, 1960, I was interviewed by a rather skeptical reporter. He asked me if I could foretell the winner of the presidential election in November of that year. I informed him that I knew nothing whatsoever about American politics, but that if he wanted to bring me a list of possible candidates, I would make my selection.

At the same time, I told him he was a very lucky man to be sitting there talking to me in my apartment that morning, because he had recently had a rather serious operation on his chest, and even though I felt that there was a nasty scar left from the operation, he was now a fit man.

He looked slightly shocked and said, "I have heard about your powers, Mr. Woodruff, but until this moment I was a skeptic. You did not know that I have only been out of the hospital for two months, having undergone a serious operation on my chest and abdomen for cancer. And you are so right when you say how very lucky I am to be here today."

The same reporter returned that afternoon and handed me a list. My eyes immediately rested on one name and I felt it was the one I was compelled to select; it was Senator John Kennedy. Accordingly, I informed him that Kennedy would win. The next morning the *Los Angeles Mirror* carried banner headlines: "It is in the stars for Kennedy."

At that time, the late President Kennedy had not even been nominated. A few weeks later I repeated this prediction on television. After that I began to notice that nearly everyone I met, including Ann and Jack Warner, seemed to have his money on Nixon. I found people coming up to me at parties shaking their heads sadly over my ignorance of the American scene.

I have to admit now that as I sat in front of the television set in my Hollywood apartment on that November election day and listened to the reports of the photo finish voting, I began to wonder whether perhaps this time I had stuck the Woodruff neck out just a little too far.

Happily my gift had not failed me. When an excited announcer appeared on the screen, I knew with absolute certainty that he was going to say, "Kennedy wins."

Over the years I have learned to turn my gift on and

Probing the Unknown

off at will. Otherwise, I would wear myself out and have nothing left to give to the people who come to me for advice. Yet there are times when I find that a total stranger's problems in some way force themselves into my mind so strongly that I feel compelled to help. On Easter, 1969, I was riding in a taxi in New York when I felt I had to speak to the driver—he had, of course, recognized me from my television series.

"You're depressed, aren't you?" I said. "For years you and your wife have been longing to have a family, but now you think you are both getting too old for one."

He stopped the cab suddenly and turned around. "Good Lord, how did you know?" he asked. "You're absolutely right. As a matter of fact, we've just about given up all hope."

"Well, don't give up," I told him. "You'll probably think I'm completely mad, but if you follow my advice, I guarantee you will have a very healthy baby. You have to work very hard, and when you get home late at night you are so tired that, if you make love to your wife, she doesn't conceive. I want you to go to bed at your usual time, but set the alarm clock for two or three in the morning and make that the time for love. When you have had some rest and you then make love, knowing that you have more rest to follow, you will find your wife will conceive, and you will have a very healthy baby boy."

He wrote to me at the studio and told me some three months later that he had taken my advice, and his wife was now pregnant and feeling fine. I never did learn whether the baby was a boy or a girl.

I can appreciate that it is difficult to grasp the gift or the power of clairvoyancy, even if you accept the fact that it does operate. You may well find it hard to believe that it works at a range of thousands of miles, the more so when someone is involved whom I have never even met. Yet it does work and I have proven it again and again.

For example, in December, 1961, I went to Los Angeles to write the script of a long-playing record for Warner Brothers on which I was to make a number of international predictions for the coming year. One of these predictions was that Elizabeth Taylor would soon be as near to death as any star had ever been.

Shortly before we made the actual recording I flew to New York for two weeks and one evening I received a telephone call from one of the executives of Warner Records in Hollywood. He said, "Have you heard the news, Maurice? Elizabeth Taylor's dying."

"No, she's not," I replied. "Will you please take another look at my script? I said she would be near to death." It is, of course, past history now that at that time Elizabeth Taylor was taken very ill in London, and it was thought she would die of pneumonia. It was only through the skill of a very famous surgeon who performed a tracheotomy on her that she recovered, but there was no doubt at all that she had been very near to death.

There has always been an imp of mischief in me, and I admit that I enjoy convincing people who are skeptical about clairvoyance, though not as painfully as I convinced the late Alma Cogen. Alma was a top singing star in Great Britain, and was known all over the world. When she first came to me she was absolutely dubious about my psychic gift. She was of a different opinion after being kept awake by a raging toothache within a day of my telling her that she should see a dentist as soon as possible.

It also gives me the greatest pleasure and satisfaction to be able to stop someone from worrying or fretting

Probing the Unknown

needlessly over a situation, by showing him as clearly as I can what will really happen. I have in front of me a letter from a twenty-two-year-old typist who lives in Massachusetts:

> I have been engaged to marry for just over a year, and all that time I have had something wrong with my legs. Now my fiancé is really pressing me to set the wedding date. Although I love him, I am beginning to wonder whether or not I have done the wrong thing in becoming engaged. I really am afraid that the condition of my legs will never improve, and that this will make our union in marriage an unhappy one. My fiancé keeps reassuring me and saying that it will make no difference, but I really cannot rid myself of this perpetual fear.

Now, this is a type of obsession that crops up quite often in people's letters. A person can be convinced that he is ugly, or lacks a vivacious personality, or has some physical defect, when nine times out of ten there really is no foundation at all for this worry. Yet it can grow out of all proportion and wreck his chances of romance, or marriage.

In this particular case, the girl has not told me exactly what is wrong with her legs, but as a clairvoyant I know that she is simply very prone to cramps. I would stake my reputation on the fact that at some time she overheard either her mother or father insulting the other by saying that their daughter was ugly or had a physical blemish. Of course, this may have happened so long ago that the girl has completely forgotten it, but she is subconsciously terrified that, if and when she marries, there may come a time when her husband will react in exactly the same way to her.

Reminiscences

In actual fact, even though she does not realize it, she is using this trouble with her legs just as an excuse to put off marriage. My advice to her is going to be: "Go ahead and marry." When she has a baby boy, as she will within eighteen months of the marriage, not only will she forget about the legs, but the cramps will vanish.

In many instances my predictions surprise me by coming true within days or even hours after they are made. But the swiftest confirmation I have yet known in my forecasting experiences involved someone's well-being and came within a matter of minutes. I was standing in the Warner Brothers studio watching Efrem Zimbalist, Jr., rehearse a rough-and-tumble fighting scene for the famous television series, "77 Sunset Strip." Efrem was close enough to overhear me ask Dorothy Atlas, Warner's press and publicity lady, if an actor ever ran into a real punch in this kind of scene.

"Very seldom," Dorothy said.

"Well," I said, "I think that they had better be careful today, because Efrem is heading for a spot of rather painful trouble."

Efrem, who is one of the nicest guys it has been my good fortune to meet, laughed at my remark. Five minutes later, when they were starting to film the scene, he was flat on his back with a beautiful black eye. As they picked him up and sent for the doctor, he turned to me and said, "There ought to be a law against letting clairvoyants into these studios!"

One of the strange things about clairvoyancy is that on rare occasions I will find such an unlikely vision of the future coming into my mind that I am almost unable to interpret it.

Probing the Unknown

Roger Moore, who plays the Saint in the TV series, has long been a very good friend of mine. Some while ago I was lunching with him in Hollywood when I had a sudden impression of him filming in unbearable heat.

"It is going to be so bad," I warned him, "that you will be quite ill all the way through the shooting of the film."

Neither Roger nor I could imagine anything hotter than Hollywood was at that particular time, but shortly afterward Roger signed a new contract and found himself filming on location in the notorious Death Valley, one of the hottest places on earth. Roger was taken sick on the first day, and from then on he was compelled to spend all his time between scenes lying in a portable dressing room with ice bags packed completely around his head.

I do not claim that I am always right with every prediction I make, because that would be nothing short of miraculous. Sometimes my statements turn out to be wide of the mark, even though I was absolutely certain when I made them. Nevertheless, events have proved me right 75 percent of the time, though a clairvoyant, no matter what his standing, can run into embarrassing situations even by being correct.

For instance, just after World War II, I was standing talking to a complete stranger at a party when quite suddenly I found myself asking, "Tell me, what was that trouble your brother had with his neck?" He turned abruptly on his heel and walked away, obviously shaken.

My host told me afterward, "Didn't you know that his brother was hanged?"

I can recall a winter's afternoon on a school recreation ground when another young boy and I were arguing about who owned a football. Quite suddenly I lost my temper; into my mind flashed a very clear picture of this young lad scratching himself, and I got a sharp impression of sickness.

Before I knew what I was saying, I had blurted out, "You'll get chicken pox tomorrow, and it'll serve you right!"

The very next morning he was absent from school with chicken pox.

As early as nine years of age, I realized for the first time that I had inherited the psychic gift that had made my late mother, Vera Woodruff, the most famous clairvoyant in Edwardian society. In the years since then, ill health has been one of the problems quite often brought to me by my private clients and by newspaper and magazine readers alike.

When I am face to face with someone, it is the eyes that tell me all I need to know about his past and future, and the eyes are really never more expressive than where his health is concerned.

As I have said, in 1957 when I was giving readings to the celebrity guests at London's Café de Paris, among the international stars who performed there was film actor and singer Carl Brisson. Carl, the father of American producer Frederick Brisson, was a man who always looked superbly fit, and he was very proud of this. But when I looked at him, he worried me. I could see in his eyes that tragedy was near. One evening, as we were chattering together while he waited to give his performance, I was startled to see the tanned, alert face in front of me change for a split second into that of an old man.

I put it down to some trick of lighting. But when we met again after he had done his show, I studied him rather closely, and again this overwhelming impression of old age came over me.

As gently as I could, I warned him. "You know," I said, "you really must take it easier. I'm not at all happy about your health."

He laughed heartily. "Me?" There and then, to the surprise of the elegant patrons crowding the lounge, he did a brisk series of exercises. "I'm sorry, Mr. Woodruff," he said. "You are rather wide of the mark this time."

A couple of months later he suddenly collapsed and died.

In this case I worked through the eyes, and for this reason I prefer to meet someone in person. But I can also tell a great deal, through a letter, about its writer's real state of health. To a certain extent this is simply observation, which anyone can try to do. If you find that the handwriting slopes backward and forward in the course of a single sentence, and if the actual phrasing varies between clear and woolly, then there must be something wrong.

I believe that worry is a state of health as well as a state of mind, for worry can quite literally get you down. If your nerves are in a turmoil, every part of you is upset, and while you are worrying you cannot possibly think clearly. The soundest possible advice I could ever give to you is, "Sleep on it," and if you have a worry on your mind, you will then find this simple trick does help tremendously. While you are worrying, your mind cannot possibly be thinking clearly for you. When you go to bed, a good exercise is to lie on your left side until you become drowsy, then turn on your back until you become even more drowsy, and finally tell yourself that you are going to sleep on your right side.

You will be so busy concentrating on this little exercise that you will find you are not brooding on the thoughts spinning around in your mind. After you have had a good night's sleep, you should be able to tackle your problems with a very clear head. Again, remember that all the while you worry, your mind cannot possibly be thinking clearly.

I recall dining one evening in Hollywood with Jack Warner, who was then one of the world's most powerful movie tycoons. During the course of conversation I made some comment about the luxury of his house and he said, "It's luxurious, yes, but I worked damned hard for it. Do you know that when we first started, we had one small ramshackle movie house and it was my job to go out in front and keep the audience happy while my brother was changing the reels?"

It has always been my opinion that hard work can be an attitude of mind, as well as a means to the end of making money. When we meet wealthy people, most of us are naturally curious about the way they spend their money. If they are a little mean, or are not as free with it as we imagine that we would be in their position, we rather tend to interpret this as being tightfisted.

Most certainly the borderline between being mean and being careful is a very, very narrow one, but when I come across people who are apparently mean, I feel very sorry for them. My work tells me that almost without exception it was some hardship they met earlier in life that has given them a mental quirk about money.

One summer day during the early years of my career, I was, asked to visit a Mrs. X who lived in a rather seedy quarter of London. I had been told that she was an extremely wealthy widow, but her house was small and

Probing the Unknown

shabby, as she was herself, and what little furniture I would see was decrepit and old-fashioned. Thus, if she was wealthy, she clearly spent very little of her money.

However, when I walked into her sitting room, I found that despite the sunshine outside, a big coal fire was blazing in the grate. The room itself was crammed with more valuable paintings than I have ever seen outside an art museum.

Mrs. X, I learned, wanted to consult me about some family matter that neither her solicitor nor she could figure out, and after I had advised her she asked me to stay to tea.

I liked her, and I was curious about her background because, apart from this strange house, when I looked into her eyes I had a very unusual sensation of suffering linked to intense cold at some stage in her past. As we talked, I discovered that she had been brought up in an orphanage and had left the orphanage to go on the stage. While she was still in her teens, she had known real poverty, living in cheap rooms in London's East End, often going very short of food and sleeping on a bed covered with newspapers.

Eventually she began to make a decent living as a chorus girl. As she danced in a musical show one night, she caught the eye of a very prosperous stockbroker, and within the space of two weeks they were married.

When her husband died at quite an early age, she inherited a very large fortune in investments. Not having great business sense herself and being scared that a stock market crash might plunge her back into poverty, she sold the shares and also her big country house. She put almost all of her money into the purchase of paintings—this was the one form of capital she regarded as safe. She

Reminiscences

lived alone, quite frugally, but was passionately determined never again to be without warmth or money.

The lure of something for nothing has brought me some very strange requests in my time. Some friends of mine who purchased a very old manor house in England, originally owned by the Duke of Norfolk, discovered that, according to local legend and the British Museum, this house had been owned by monks in the fifteenth century. The monks had built a chapel under what was now the lounge, and after the monks had been driven out by King Henry VIII, the Knights of the Order of Saint John of Jerusalem took over the manor house. In this medieval chapel were buried those knights who died, wearing their full armor and, so the story went, their gold and jewels buried with them.

My friends who now owned the house reasoned that the burial place must be beneath their marble-floored hall, and they started digging with a pickax and a shovel. The net result of their labor was a ruined marble floor.

They telephoned me and asked me down for the weekend in the hope that I could find the right spot.

Feeling rather foolish, I said, "I think you will find it's under that rosebush by the gate at the back of your house which leads on outside the lounge."

The treasure hunters rushed for their spades and found a charnel pit filled with human bones in that spot.

I do not claim to be infallible. If I were ever tempted to do so, I would only have to remember the comment made by the famous English novelist Olga Stringfellow when a newspaper reporter telephoned and asked her what she would do if the four-minute end-of-the-world warning sounded.

Probing the Unknown

"*I'd telephone Maurice Woodruff,*" said Olga, "*and ask for my money back!*"

In 1960 a client whose name was Sam Poppy came to me. During the reading I was slightly confused because I could see hair all around him, for both men and women. I told him that he would work either with or for someone who had something to do with the United States Senate, but that after a while he would leave this man and go into business on his own.

Shortly after this reading Sam Poppy joined ex-Senator Glen Taylor, who had found a new means of making hairpieces for bald men. Sam, who had been a first-class hairdresser for most of his life, worked with Taylor for some time, after which Sam decided to go on his own. He had discovered a different way of making hairpieces, not on a separate base but by taking a black man's hair and weaving strips of it onto his skull. This method, of course, spread exactly as I had predicted to white men and women. Also, one could say that Sam Poppy played a large part in starting the wig business in major stores throughout the United States.

Arlene Dahl has long been a very dear friend of mine, and both in Hollywood and in New York she has kindly given dinner parties for me. I well remember going to one where a rather beautiful blonde lady, whose name I did not even know, asked me if I could tell her something about herself. I did not want to take the glory of the evening from the guests of honor, but felt compelled to tell this lady that she had been the victim of a robbery and had lost a lot of valuable jewelry. I described the way her house was laid out and the man who I thought had been the thief and who had enjoyed the assistance of another person who was working in her house at the time.

Reminiscences

Unfortunately I had to tell her that she would not get her jewelry back.

At the same time, I looked at her husband and said he owned a horse that would be racing the next day, and that the horse would come in either first or second.

Senator Jacob Javits and Burt Bacharach said to me, "Don't say that, Maurice, because we like you, and don't want to see you make a bad prediction. This horse is a rank outsider."

But Angie Dickinson (Mrs. Burt Bacharach), who is an old friend of mine, said, "If you are serious about this, Maurice, then Burt and I will place a bet on it."

The gentleman in question, who was Cornelius Vanderbilt (Sonny) Whitney, said that if I was right, he would feel too sick to lead his horse in, even if it were to win.

His wife, Mary Lou Whitney, then told me that she had indeed been burgled and had lost quite a lot of jewelry in that year—1967—and admitted that my description of her house and rooms was staggeringly accurate.

The following evening I telephoned Mr. Whitney and asked how his horse had run. He told me that, in fact, it had come in first, and that he had been so unwell he could not lead it in. Regarding Mrs. Whitney's jewelry, I never did learn whether or not she ever got any of it back.

Quite often I am asked whether my gift is thought-reading or telepathy. Well, of course, it is neither of these things. I can tell you about something and describe it fully when it is not even in your mind or has long since been forgotten, and I am able to predict future events for you of which you have no plan or idea. This most certainly cannot be either thought-reading or telepathy.

When I made a long-playing record for my old friend

Probing the Unknown

Robert Weiss at Warner Records, I predicted that there would be a new star on Broadway in the year 1963. I remember saying that she would most certainly not make it by her looks, but by her singular talent that involved a truly magical voice. I also stated that there would be an initial B around her name.

When I arrived in New York in 1963 with my manager, I had a call from a friend, Helen Winston, and she said, "Maurice, I want you and Harry to come along with my husband and myself tonight. They are doing a preview of *Funny Girl* at the Winter Garden theater, and I feel sure this is the girl involved in your prediction on your Warner's album two years ago. She does not have good looks, but has a fantastic voice, and I am told is extremely talented. Her name is Barbra Streisand."

6.

Reincarnation (Immortality)

How often have you read that this or that person is almost immortal? And how often does immortality become confused with reincarnation?

A person who has written a special book or musical composition, or has been saintlike in his behavior, does, in effect, become immortal, but it is only what he has contributed to the world as a person that forms the basis of this immortality. In other words, one might be remembered throughout history, and revered, but not necessarily be reincarnated.

I personally have never doubted the actuality of reincarnation. It is my conviction that there are very few new souls on earth. If we accept the fact that the earth is round, then at one end of the earth's circumference is point A, and at the other end point B. Thus you enter life at point A, and always, provided you live a normal existence, you move to point B, where, for want of a better word, you pass away. From point B around again to point A, you are resting and ridding yourself of your earthly cares and worries and ills, so that you enter point A again as a refreshed soul.

This does not necessarily mean that you would come back to the same family. It is my belief that we come back to point A many, many times. Accordingly, the expression "I have been here before," to my way of thinking, holds more truth than most people ever imagine. How often have you gone into a place for the very first time and subconsciously known, without a single doubt in your mind, that you have been there before, but cannot say why you know this?

An example of this occurred many years ago when a young English society boy, a friend of mine named Evelyn Pixley, was invited by a group of friends to accompany them to Versailles. Quite naturally while at Versailles they were taken on a guided tour of the palace of Louis XIV. Going through one of the galleries, the guide pointed out certain very old and very precious tapestries that were hanging on the walls alongside priceless paintings and art treasures.

Suddenly, for no apparent reason, Evelyn blurted out, "Well, I want to see inside the room that is behind that tapestry!"

The guide looked surprised and hastened to assure Evelyn and his friends that there was no room behind that tapestry.

Evelyn quickly replied, "Oh, but there is, and I can describe it to you in detail," and he went on to describe the room and its contents.

The guide looked at the others as though Evelyn was demented and said that, since they were nearing the end

Reincarnation (Immortality)

of their tour, they had better push on in order to complete it before the palace was closed for the day.

Nothing more was said until they reached the end of the tour, when the guide took Evelyn by the arm and quietly asked him if he and his two friends would stay behind after the others had gone. Being intrigued, they agreed. After the other members of the tour had departed, the guide then asked Evelyn how he knew there was a room behind the tapestry. Evelyn could only say that he did not understand how he knew, but that he just knew. The guide then took them up to the gallery and lifted the tapestry, behind which was a door. He unlocked the door and took them into a room that was, in actual fact, exactly as Evelyn Pixley had described it. I might add here that until that day Evelyn Pixley had never been abroad, had never left the shores of England, his native country. He did not have X-ray eyes or an extraordinary imagination.

Such incidents, of course, occur very frequently in people's lives. They have a feeling they have met complete strangers before, and no doubt they have, but in a former existence. Although it sounds rather simplistic, I believe that we live this life and progress or retard in our next life according to our behavior. I also believe that we return many, many times, and this is why our memories play tricks with us on rare occasions.

In all seriousness a person may tell me that he often has the feeling of having lived in Egyptian times, or Victorian times. I never scoff at this. I myself, as a tiny child, could describe to my mother and brothers and sister a mid-Victorian drawing room to perfection. The late Sir Winston Churchill's mother, who was a client and friend of my mother, was very interested in the subject. She was of the opinion that I had lived in mid-Victorian days and had died very young in my previous life. This would

Probing the Unknown

have accounted for the fact that I was able to describe an age that was not so very many years removed from the year of my birth, 1916.

There are, of course, spirits who are known as halfways, but these have no connection with reincarnation. It has been explained that these are people who died an unnatural death before their life span was completed. They have either taken their own lives or met with accidents, and therefore appear unable to settle down. This must come under the heading of spiritualism, a science in which I firmly believe, but have not explored extensively. I usually advise any of my friends who may be interested in spiritualism not to dabble in it without investigation of all its many manifestations and effects.

Many of the world's great religious leaders have, in their time, taught the philosophy of rebirth, which really is the theory of reincarnation and derives mostly from the Eastern nations. I myself have spent some time in different parts of the world, among them Morocco. I can assure you that very few Moroccans would reject the theory that one returns after death to a new life. They believe very firmly indeed in the doctrine of Karma, which teaches that most of us are responsible for our deeds through all eternity.

In England there was a girl named Anne Ockendan who was put into a hypnotic trance and in actual fact was taken back through many, many lives. She was only a country girl with no great command of the English language, but when under the trance she spoke French, Hebrew, German, and Chinese fluently. She described where she had lived in China over two hundred years before and even was able to recall her former names.

Reincarnation (Immortality)

The hypnotist, who was a doctor and philosopher, traveled many miles to check on her statements, and through records he found that such places and names still existed. She left no doubt about her statements under hypnotic trance because she spoke with such great clarity, and she also not only spoke the languages fluently but behaved as people did in each particular time so many years ago.

I learned of Anne Ockendan's story when I was doing a television series in Wales in 1961. During a program I went over to a member of my audience, a lady in her fifties, and told her that she had written a book. I also mentioned that after writing it she had realized that there must be a second book to complete her story, and in fact she had not written the book herself but a man with white hair had begun the writing of this book with the help of a young girl.

The lady became so excited that she jumped up in her seat in full view of the camera and cried, "Oh, yes! You are so right, Mr. Woodruff. I had a book published in October, 1960, and am now writing a second one."

When my show finished that evening, many people from the audience rushed forward to ask me questions, as is usual every time I do a program. Among these individuals was a very short, white-haired man, obviously in his mid-sixties, who said to me, "Mr. Woodruff, you were so uncanny with that lady who, you said, had written the book. I am the white-haired man who instigated the writing. I am her doctor, and I will send you the book if you give me your address." I gave it to him, and eventually received the book, which was entitled *Who Was Anne Ockendan?*

Even the most skeptical of us cannot with honesty

Probing the Unknown

deny reincarnation. Throughout our entire lives we appear to be looking forward at all times to something, and even the dying person recognizes this just at the point of death.

I was with my late manager, Bill Thomas, when he died, and two things occurred at his death. First, a few seconds before he died, his eyes opened quite wide and a happy look came over his face, as though he had recognized someone. Second, at the moment of his death all the lines and cares in his face (he had been ill for quite a long period of time) did in fact completely go, and in his composed state he looked at least ten years younger.

One of the greatest men it has been my privilege to meet was the late British Air Chief Marshal, Lord Dowding, who headed the Royal Air Force during World War II. He was known to his intimates as "Stuffy" Dowding. He became a very great spiritualist who believed very strongly not only in life after death, but in reincarnation. He wrote a book in layman's language on the subject, which everybody found very easy to understand because it had none of the great technical details that I believe quite often puzzle readers.

He told me that he had had many experiences, and the beginning of his interest in reincarnation was caused by the loss of his son. He had been able to communicate with young men who had been killed while serving under his command. He said that in many cases an airman who had been mortally wounded would stand looking at himself wherever he lay and watch those near and dear grieving over their loss.

Lord Dowding explained that these spirits had described the situation to him. Once they had passed over, they fell

Reincarnation (Immortality)

asleep for some time (remember that time has no meaning beyond), and would sleep away their earthly aches and pains, illnesses, or the damage done to them, in order to effect an early demise. After this sleep, they would wake up refreshed and enter into another dimension where they would await their return once again into this life, not necessarily to the same family.

Lord Dowding quite often attended spiritualist meetings, and was at one time accused of being a crank. If you had met this great man, you would never have agreed with that accusation. Not only was he a brilliant leader of men during wartime, but basically he was a wonderful, understanding person.

When Lord Dowding died in 1969 newspapers throughout the world, and many people who at one time had accused him of being a "crank," withdrew their nasty remarks. The press, with one accord, heaped many accolades upon him. Even the late Sir Winston Churchill was criticized for his treatment of this great man.

The late great author, Sir Arthur Conan Doyle, so believed in both spiritualism and reincarnation that he formed a pact during his lifetime with the late journalist, Hannan Swaffer. He predicted that he would come back and give Hannan news from the other side. I never did find out whether this ever happened because I never had the opportunity of meeting either of these great gentlemen. I do know that Hannan Swaffer formed a friendship with the editor of the famous British newspaper, *The Psychic News*, Maurice Barbinel, and this gentleman in particular has carried on this great work through the medium of his newspaper.

As we all so well remember, the late Bishop James Pike, who started life as a lawyer and then became a priest, believed in spiritualism. It was only after the loss of his son that he let the world know how much he had become involved in spiritualism and in reincarnation.

Yes, I certainly do believe in reincarnation.

My Spiritual Experiences

How often have you heard someone say that he has either seen or heard a ghost, and your reaction has been that this is rubbish? Well, as I have always advocated, everybody is entitled to his beliefs or disbeliefs, and one should go by his own experiences.

Let me first make it quite clear that I am not a spiritualist, but I do believe in life after death and in reincarnation. On many occasions I have been involved in both humorous and eerie experiences with spirits who have passed on.

When I was a small child of nine years, my late mother, Vera Woodruff, my sister, Phyllis, and I lived in an apartment in the St. Johns Wood district of London. The apartment was on the top floor of a four-story house. We had just sacked our maid, and my mother was on her hands and knees cleaning and polishing the fireplace in the drawing room, when a knock came at the door.

Without looking up, my mother said, "Come in."

There was no response and nobody entered, yet the knock came again. Once more my mother, without turning around, told the person to enter.

Again there was no response, and so my mother answered the knock by saying, "Well, if you don't want to come in, don't keep knocking."

As she said this, she turned around and looked at the door. Mother saw a mist in the form of a figure; she sank back on her heels, aghast. At that moment I was coming up the stairs and saw for myself the figure coming down

Reincarnation (Immortality)

the staircase. Minutes later, the woman who lived on the floor below let out a very loud scream. She, too, had seen the mist going past her landing. We learned much later on that many years before another clairvoyant had owned the house. We never ascertained whether or not the spirit belonged to this clairvoyant.

When I was seventeen, I had my own apartment in Highgate, London. It was from this historical area that Dick Whittington and his famous black cat had walked into the center of London to be proclaimed its first Lord Mayor. I often heard strange noises from the floor above me, yet I knew that floor to be empty of people and furniture. I asked my landlord about the noises but he would always reply that it was my imagination. However, I am not a person who is given to wild fantasies.

At one period in 1947, the landlord had plumbers in the house to do some repiping, and a temporary water tap was installed mid-stairs. I came in late one night and, as was my usual custom, I went mid-stairs to the temporary tap to fill a kettle for a cup of tea. Suddenly, standing there alone, I felt a cold wind on my back, heard a faint noise, and felt myself being pushed on to the tap itself. Nobody was there, and I can tell you I was thoroughly frightened.

I dropped the kettle and ran like hell.

The next day I told my landlord about my experience and asked him if my imagination could have caused it. He then told me truthfully there was no one living upstairs. However, an old lady had lived alone there for many years. She had died four years before, and a considerable time had elapsed before anyone found her. He asked me not to tell the other tenants because he did not want to alarm them. I most certainly did not tell them. I moved out the very next day.

My present home is quite beautiful, with grounds and

stables, and is located in Kent, a section that is regarded as the garden of England. The dwelling was built originally in the year 1452 and has lots of character, with old beams and so on, and although central heating and air conditioning have been installed, it still has all its original charm. After I bought the house and had moved in, I was sitting in one of the lounges watching television one night. My manager, Harry Arnold, who was with me, said he could hear noises upstairs and he thought we must have burglars.

I also heard the noise, and while I am not all that brave, I am curious. Accordingly, I got up and climbed the first staircase and looked into all the bedrooms and the bathroom, and then turned around to come downstairs in order to get to the second staircase to the other wing of the house. Since very thick carpet covers most of the floors, I did not realize that Harry Arnold was behind me, following me all the way. You can imagine my shock when I turned around and saw him standing there. My reaction scared him, but we eventually laughed over this incident. There were no burglars, but we eventually got used to hearing the noise of someone walking about upstairs at night.

In 1967, I gave a very large party at the house, and included in the guests were the mayor and mayoress of the district. Pauline Chalk, the mayoress, quite suddenly asked me if I had ever seen the ghost of our house, and I asked her what ghost she was talking about.

"Didn't you know that your house has been quite famous for its ghost throughout history, Maurice?" she asked me.

I said that I had not been aware of this, and she informed me that a man had hanged himself in the late fifteenth century in one of the upstairs bedrooms. I asked her to show

Reincarnation (Immortality)

me that particular bedroom and, as it turned out, it was the room in which Judy Garland was sleeping that night. Judy and I often laughed about this later. While I am very much aware that this ghost does in fact exist, it is a very happy house, and my ghost obviously does not mean me any harm.

Quite a few years ago a client who has been coming to me for many years arrived for one of his regular meetings. This client is a very successful businessman, and in fact has been called a chocolate baron. He only wanted to know about his business affairs, and I had learned from experience that I was not supposed to trespass into his personal life, no matter how much I wanted to or how pressing the matter might be.

On this particular occasion, however, I did just that thing, because I had such a strong compulsion. I informed him that I thought he must have had a child around the age of eleven or twelve years, who I thought was a girl, and that he had lost her. Although she appeared to me to be very wet, she had not drowned. I also had the distinct impression that either he or his wife, or both, had, in effect, almost accused the child of doing something wrong before they lost her. I added that within two years from the date of this particular reading, it would be proved to him how wrong was his accusation. My client went rather white in the face, and I mistakenly judged this to be a reaction of anger at my intruding into the domestic side of his life.

Three years later the baron came to see me again (he had, of course, been coming very regularly during those three years, and even had me flown across the Continent to give him readings when it was not convenient for him to visit London).

Probing the Unknown

This time, as he sat down, he said to me, "You know, Mr. Woodruff, you really are rather remarkable. I am not going to try to fool you, because I have consulted quite a few clairvoyants throughout the world in my travels, but have so far found you to be the most correct. You may remember telling me some three years ago that you thought I had a child, a girl, aged around eleven or twelve, and that you thought I had lost her, and that she was wet, but had not drowned.

"You also said that within two years it would be proved to my wife and myself that we had accused our daughter falsely of something. Well, it is three years, not two, and we have just been through the most harrowing experience of our lives and never wish to have it repeated. But I must tell you how right you were.

"In actual fact, we did have a little girl, and on her twelfth birthday my wife and I decided to buy her a really fine gift. We went to Cartier's and had a locket made for her to wear around her neck. Naturally, when she received this on her birthday, she was delighted.

"We were down at our country house in England—it was quite a large manor house—and the lounge leads out via a French window onto lawns which, in turn, lead downhill to a lake. Our daughter had been having a very happy birthday. When she came in that summer evening the first thing my wife noticed was that she was not wearing the locket. Quite naturally she asked her what she had done with it.

"Our beautiful little girl looked surprised and alarmed, put her hand up to her neck, and said, 'Oh, Mummy! I must have lost it, but I promise you the clasp was weak, because I intended to show it to you and Daddy when I came in.' My wife was a little angry, and I gave her my support because, after all, we had spent a lot of money for the locket. My daughter was ordered up to her room at once.

"About eight o'clock that evening I told my wife that our daughter had been punished enough, and my wife agreed. Together we took her dinner up to her bedroom and found her missing. We immediately thought she was sulking, that she would get over it and would come out from wherever she was hiding in time. At ten o'clock that night we began to be worried when suddenly the French windows of our lounge opened, and there stood my little girl dripping with water from head to foot. She was crying, and protested that she had done her best but could not find the locket. Again she said that the clasp was broken; she was not telling a lie!

"Now, if you think, Mr. Woodruff, that we were accusing our daughter from then on, you are quite mistaken. All thought of the missing locket was banished from our minds. We rushed our daughter upstairs and gave her a hot bath. After we had persuaded her to take a hot drink we put her to bed and soothed her. Unfortunately she had caught a cold which tragically turned into pneumonia, and we lost her; it almost broke my wife's heart.

"We have not gone to the country house since then, but one month ago we were deciding that either we must use the house on weekends or sell it. Since it is such a lovely house, we decided to start going there once again, and to spend some time there.

"When we arrived, there were new tradesmen and our servants had been changed. Even the old gardener had retired and a new young one had taken his place. Shortly after we had settled in, our housekeeper informed us that a young child was missing in the district (remember that this is only a small country village). The child's description had been given out, so that if anybody saw her they could either telephone or get in touch with her parents or the police. We did not take a great deal of notice about this event.

"At four o'clock that afternoon, however, the little girl who had been lost walked in through the open French windows of our lounge. We knew at once who she was, but the alarming thing was that she addressed my wife as Mummy, and me as Daddy.

"She also knew all of our little girl's hiding places, and even where our child had hung her hat and coat. She called by name the old tradespeople and all our old servants. My wife, meanwhile, was becoming rather emotionally upset. We immediately sent our gardener to notify the child's parents and at the same time telephoned the local doctor who had attended both us and our daughter.

"Quite horrifyingly, when the child's parents arrived she was extremely polite to them as though they were strangers, and still kept referring to my wife and myself as Mummy and Daddy. The doctor suggested that possibly she had been wandering for a couple of days and was in a state of shock, and (knowing what had happened to our own child) asked if we would mind putting the youngster up for just one night. He was reasonably certain that, with a fairly strong sedative, she would sleep well and be her old self by the next morning. Naturally, we agreed to do this. I do not have to tell you, however, how upset her parents were. And my wife, I can assure you, Mr. Woodruff, was almost completely distraught by this time.

"At nine o'clock that night the doctor returned to see the girl and give her another sedative. When we went up to her room, however, we were all shocked to find her missing. There was no way to account for her absence. We are not drinking folk, but I suggested that we should go down to the lounge and have a drink.

"Then, at exactly ten o'clock that evening (the same time as our own daughter had appeared that night three years ago), our French windows opened and this child walked in, dripping from head to foot with water and dangling a locket from her hand.

"She looked at my wife and said, 'You see, Mummy, I *was* being truthful. The clasp was broken!' My wife fainted, and the child's real mother became hysterical. The little girl was taken upstairs, given a hot bath and a hot drink, exactly as had been done for our child, and put to bed with a sedative from the doctor.

"The next morning she awoke, opened her eyes, and immediately asked for her mother and father, who were there and greatly relieved to see that she recognized them. She was quite her old self again, and they took her home.

"We have now decided quite definitely to sell this house, because I can assure you, Mr. Woodruff, that my wife and I never want to go through such an experience ever again. I am only telling you this story now to show you how right you were, even if you were just one year out in time."

My former manager, Bill Thomas, was a wonderful man who died, unfortunately, in 1963. I remember a story about him that occurred way back in 1952. Bill got slightly worried about the health of his father, who lived in North Wales. We were living in London at the time and Bill wondered, in effect, how much longer his elderly father would last; he asked me if I could tell him. I felt that Bill

Probing the Unknown

should pay a visit to my mother, Vera Woodruff, for a reading because I was too close to him. Seeing him almost every day might make me wrong.

As directed, he went along to see my mother. When he returned, I asked him what she had said, and he indicated my mother had told him that his father would live for a few more years, but when eventually he did die it would be in the spring of the year.

Feeling rather mischievous at the time, I said that I disagreed; I thought his father would last just two more years, and that in the spring of the year he would be coming down a hill, to a pub at the bottom, for a drink of beer. He would be taken ill on the way and would be brought to a neighbor's house, and then taken back uphill to his own house, where he would recover after a rest. By the time the leaves fell from the trees in the fall of that year, he would make his last walk down the hill, and Bill Thomas would then lose him. After I said this, we both forgot about it.

In my bedroom in those days I had a divan with a table beside it on which stood a telephone, in case there should be any calls during the night (which of course I discouraged). In early September, two years later, I was awakened in the night by three rather sharp raps on that table, and I immediately thought I had burglars in the house.

I then remembered that I had been told some years before by a friend of mine who was a spiritualist medium that if ever I heard such a thing, I should remain calm and just say, "Can I help you, friend?"

Having an extremely wicked sense of humor, I lay there thinking to myself, "You're going to feel pretty stupid talking into a dark room, and saying, 'Can I help you, friend?' when there is no one there to be seen."

Reincarnation (Immortality)

After a while I began to think I must have imagined the knocking. Suddenly, once again three very loud raps came upon that table. I was much younger in those days and did not like this experience very much. I decided that, instead of asking whether I could help, I had better put the sheets over my head and go back to sleep.

The next morning at breakfast I told Bill Thomas of my experience. It also occurred to me that he really ought to try to get in touch with his father to see if he was all right. As it happened, his father had passed away during the previous night, possibly at the time I heard those raps on my table.

You may or may not have read about a very famous English house, Borley Rectory, that was built in the fourteenth century. It was pulled down within the last twenty years. Priests used to live there, and there was always a nun in attendance. During the course of many years at least three of these nuns lost their lives in the house under what have been described as unnatural circumstances.

It was said that one of the nuns came back and regularly haunted the house. No vicar would live in the rectory for too long a period because it made his family too nervous. There would be screams, rushes of wind, and doors opening without anybody being present.

When I was in my early twenties and quite reckless, several friends and I attended a charity ball in London. Afterward, on a dare, we decided to drive down to Borley Rectory and have a look for ourselves. On the way, one of my friends, who was a burly six-foot athlete, said he thought the stories about the house were rubbish. It was ridiculous, in his opinion, even to think that such a place could be haunted by spirits. Of course we all laughed and giggled as youngsters usually do.

Probing the Unknown

When we arrived at the rectory I said to my friend, "Well, if you don't believe, and you think it's rubbish, you go round the house from the lefthand side, and we three (there were two girls with us) will go around on the right side. We'll meet again here at the front."

I must say that the two girls and I ran around the outside of the house so fast that I don't think we had time to see or even hear the spirits. When my friend met us, he was a mass of perspiration, his bow tie was opened at the neck, and he looked terrified.

"I never want to have that experience again," he said. "As soon as I started to walk around the opposite side from you three, I not only felt deadly cold [and this was summer], but I felt a great pressure upon my head as though someone was trying to push me downward. This, in turn, slowed me up and, even though I have not cried for several years, I could not get my breath to shout out, but there were, without a doubt, tears in my eyes." Indeed we three saw there were tears, and we were a very quiet foursome as we drove back to London.

Several years later it was decided to pull down the rectory because it had fallen into a state of bad repair. Every time anybody has tried to build on that land since then a situation has occurred to prevent it. No one has yet been able to complete a building on the land, although priests have tried to bless and exorcise it.

I went to live with my mother in her St. Johns Wood, London, house when I was nine years old and remained until her death. During her later years my mother became an alcoholic because her life had not been terribly happy. While she could help the many hundreds of people who came to consult her, being a psychic, she was unable to help herself. Thus, the last few years of her life were miserable ones in that house in Alexandra Road.

Reincarnation (Immortality)

Three weeks after she died I had to pay a visit to my dentist and had occasion to drive past the house. To my surprise it had burned down to the ground. I made inquiries as to what had happened and was told that there was no logical reason why the house should even have caught fire in the first instance. I have often wondered whether it was my mother's unhappy experiences that had made this come about.

7.

Clairvoyance/ Astrology and Religion

When people start talking to me about clairvoyance/astrology and religion, I must readily admit that I have rather definite opinions on these subjects. I am religious, though not a fanatic; I do believe in God; and I do know my Bible pretty well. I was taught as a child that if ever I was worried or concerned, I should turn to the ninety-first psalm; after reading it, I should have great peace of mind. I can assure you that I have abided by this regularly throughout my life.

My country house in England is just about a hundred yards down the lane from a very old church. I visit there very frequently when I am in the country, but only when I know the church will be empty, so that I may sit peacefully and pray as I wish.

I do not go there when a congregation is worshiping. We are all taught that we can sincerely say our prayers

Clairvoyance/Astrology and Religion

and they will be heard no matter whether we are in a church or a backyard. Yet when one goes to church with a congregation, invariably one knows the service, with the exception of the sermon; only once or twice throughout the year does the wording of that service change. This to me does not make sense, because I feel that the house of God should be a place where one can express what is in one's heart, not just read what is printed in a book or sing hymns that have already been written. Here is where I feel that the word *sincerity* gets lost.

Most of the churches and religions throughout the world frown upon clairvoyance and astrology. Yet we are asked to believe the Bible's accounts of Christ's miracles and the various prophets' predictions about what would happen in the future. In the Church of England and the Roman Catholic church the word spiritual is used many times throughout the service, but these churches refuse to believe in spiritualism or accept it. On the one hand, they tell us, and I believe this to be absolutely true, that Christ rose from the dead; and on the other hand they refuse to accept the fact that there is reincarnation after death. But they tell us that if we are not good in earthly life, we cannot go to heaven, which in effect is life after death.

I well remember getting into an argument many years ago with Dr. Cosmo Gordon Lang, who was at that time the Archbishop of Canterbury. We had met at a charity ball during the period of the abdication of King Edward VIII, now the Duke of Windsor.

The Archbishop said to me, "You appear to be quite an intelligent man, Mr. Woodruff. What do you think of this affair?"

My answer was, "Please do not ask me, sir, because I feel that I will shock you."

Probing the Unknown

He replied, "No, nothing shocks me very much at all, Mr. Woodruff."

I must say that he was a very wonderful man with a great sense of humor, so I said to him, "The church amazes me sometimes. If a girl is seven months pregnant you will marry her in white, but if she is one day over the pregnancy, you won't. When you marry a couple you say that, as this ring is round, so shall their love be without end. In actual fact, what is marriage other than legalized prostitution? If your wife awakens you in the middle of the night and says to you, 'Joseph, I was conceived by the Holy Ghost, and tomorrow I shall give birth to a child whom we shall name Jesus,' are you going to believe her?"

Admittedly this was facetious on my part, but I was trying to make my point to him that you cannot expect people to believe completely what they are told by the church, unless the church is willing to believe other things that do not necessarily coincide with the church's thinking.

Quite often I have had a priest or a rabbi say to me, "But this is stupid—how can one psychically see things, there is nothing to see!"

My reply is, "Well, can you see electricity in the air? Of course you can't, but you believe it to be there because scientists have told you so."

I go to church and shall still go to church because I believe very sincerely. At the same time I have faith in the gift of clairvoyance and the science of astrology. Before the church condemns this, it should start to think of putting its own house in order, especially since many major wars throughout history have been fought because of religion. Is that the teaching of the church? Surely the church cannot expect the public of today to believe things that cannot be proved absolutely, and tell them it is wrong to hold extra beliefs, such as astrology and clairvoyancy, which have enjoyed a high percentage of accurate predictions throughout the centuries.

8.

Personal Questions

People often ask me how it feels to predict important events of international and national significance.

Well, when I am appearing on the stage or television, and even when I am writing a book, my own feelings do not enter into my predictions. I realize that the world of the seventies is very fast-moving and that, in many cases, affairs can change from day to day. Thus I try to remain as neutral in my mind as is humanly possible, and then I set out to categorize the fields in which I want to make predictions.

For example, if I am concerned at the moment with such a topic as show business, science, medicine, politics, or fashion, I merely let my mind wander in that milieu and predictions just naturally come to me in the form of mental pictures. I do not look upon these predictions as

Personal Questions

great responsibilities because when I do make a definite statement, or futurecast, I must be 100 percent certain in my mind that the event will occur; otherwise I do not mention it.

I do not say to myself, "Well, that would seem a little stupid or imaginative," because I state a definite belief.

When I did Johnny Carson's "Tonight Show" in 1967, I told Johnny that Lyndon B. Johnson would announce that he was not going to run for the office of President in 1968, that the next President of the United States would be Mr. Nixon, and that Mrs. Jacqueline Kennedy would remarry.

Johnny in turn asked me what I foresaw for him, to which I replied that he would be out of his show for a short while. This made Johnny laugh, because, as we all knew, he had been doing his show for quite a few years and there was no reason why he should suddenly stop doing it. As it turned out, two or three days after I made this statement on the show, there was a strike, and this caused Johnny to be off the air for a short period.

Dorothy Manners, who writes a daily column from Hollywood about filmland and its stars, asked me for three consecutive years to predict who would win the Academy Awards. I gave her the information as requested, always quite a while before the official announcements, and my forecasts were correct. As a matter of fact, a few years ago Dorothy printed my statement that Elizabeth Taylor would win as well as her hunch that Richard Burton would win the best actor award. My prediction that year was that Paul Scofield would be the best actor, and also *A Man for All Seasons* would be the best film winner. As it turned out, all three of my predictions were accurate.

I am only human and the feelings I get when I have

made a correct prediction are quite naturally a combination of pleasure and satisfaction.

Quite often people have said to me, "But surely, if you can tell people about themselves and can also make future-casts in the international and national field, you must be able to foretell your own future."

As I have said on many occasions, I know of no genuine psychic who can honestly claim to be able to tell himself anything that affects him personally. It is a gift that is applicable only to other people. I believe that the reason a psychic cannot tell things about himself is because human nature is such a significant factor. If he had to make an unfortunate prediction for himself, the attitude of mind would be, "Oh, well, it can happen to the others, but it won't happen to me," whereas if it were a good thing the psychic would term it wishful thinking.

To illustrate this point further, when I am giving a reading or am writing a book of predictions, I *have* to be absolutely without sympathy for the person, or event, concerned. If I have sympathy, then I could prove to be wrong.

Only once have I come close to making a prediction about myself, and that was in September, 1968, when I was appearing at London's Mayfair Theatre. I was doing a show every night, two matinees a week, a late night show on Saturday, and my television series on Sunday.

One night after my stage show I was sitting in the kitchen of my London apartment and quite suddenly from out of the blue I looked up at my manager, Harry Arnold, and said, "Do you know, I have a feeling that the next two or three years are going to be spent in America for me."

Harry Arnold looked at me as though I had gone

Personal Questions

slightly mad and said, "What on earth made you say that?" because there was no reason for this to be happening.

At that time I was extremely busy in England writing for my numerous magazines and newspapers and seeing clients as well as making quite a few personal appearances. But as it turned out, at the end of September, 1968, I was asked by my American publisher to visit New York and make promotional appearances for my new book. While I was in New York I was approached by Larry Freyburg, then the head of Metromedia Television, about doing a television series the following year.

Hence I returned to England in October, came back to New York in November, made the pilot film of the show, and then came back again in early January, 1969, to commence "Maurice Woodruff Predicts." The show was put on every Saturday night in New York from 10:30 to 11:30 and was bought by stations in quite a few major cities throughout the United States.

I receive in the range of five thousand letters per week from readers of my magazine and from viewers of my television program, and I must say that I am surprised by the recurring note of self-pity in these personal questions, which, in my experience over the years, is quite new. Over and over again I come across such phrases as "I am only an ordinary person," or "I am fully aware that I am not a celebrity like most of your clients," or "Of course you would not be interested in someone like me."

I would like you to know here and now that this is simply not true. There is nothing extra special about me; I began my career as a tailor's apprentice. I am thus able to advise many "ordinary people."

I cannot help wondering why there should be this tendency to feel sorry for oneself, which is now so apparent.

Probing the Unknown

Does it, perhaps, reflect a subconscious feeling of helplessness in our age? Or could it be an increasingly materialistic outlook that makes people more envious of "them"—the people who have taken the opportunities the moaners failed to recognize? Let me quote from a letter I received from a Mr. N. of Connecticut:

> I am a stoker. For years I have been buying lottery tickets, entering competitions, without luck. My wife, two sons, and two daughters, all of school age, stay with my wife's sister and her family. At times my spirits are very low, so many things trouble me. I find that writing to you makes it easier, but I do not expect that this letter will be considered by you, because I am one of many in the working class.

Well, Mr. N., the famous English photographer, Baron Nahum, whom I have mentioned elsewhere in this book, once said to me that if you always ride on a bus, you become bus minded; if you always ride in a taxi, you become taxi minded. I say that if you keep telling yourself you are a working-class man, you will remain working-class. I felt that Mr. N. was a good worker and I knew that he had the ability to pull himself up higher on the ladder. This applies to everybody; if you sit in a rut and complain and feel sorry for yourself, you are going to stay in that rut for the rest of your life.

Neighbor trouble, housing trouble, health trouble, parent trouble, children trouble—these all keep popping up in my mail. You would be surprised how often a mother (or a father) who complains about her children reveals her own possessive nature. "Of course I never believe in interfering," she says, but surely she does interfere.

Personal Questions

In contrast, the parent who is genuinely concerned for his children's welfare deserves all the help I can give him.

I recently opened an envelope postmarked Kansas City and out of it dropped a colored photograph of an extremely attractive lady with a baby girl. The letter inside was from the baby's parent:

> My young daughter has been divorced, and twice we have both dreamt that her baby would be kidnapped, and this has now actually happened, only a few weeks after our dreams. My daughter is only twenty-one and has suffered very deeply from this. My one wish is to know if one day she will ever find true happiness. . . .

I immediately gathered from this letter that it was the child's father who had taken the baby, if that could be called kidnapping. I also felt that while this woman's daughter was very much in love with her husband, she was so possessively jealous of him she hardly ever let him out of her sight. It had obviously become more than he could stand. I wrote and told the grandmother this, but also was able to assure her that the child was being well looked after, because the father was extremely fond of her, although I could not promise that her daughter and husband would ever be reunited. The only consolation I could give the mother was the fact that her daughter would have a divorce and remarry and would then have her child back. Her marriage would be a happy one only because she would have learned the lesson that a husband can never be kept on too tight a rein.

Many people have written to ask me whether I believe in spiritualism.

My answer is always, "Yes, most certainly I do." But I

am not a practicing spiritualist, and I don't attend spiritualist meetings, because I believe quite firmly that it can too easily become an obsession.

I cite the case of one of the viewers of my recent television series in America, a lady whom I shall call Mrs. S. She told me that she had been a spiritualist for twenty years and went on:

"All my family have passed over, the last one being my dear father, who went in his sleep just before Easter. He was all I had left in life, and everything that I did was for him; now there seems no reason to carry on.

"I go to my spiritualist meetings hoping to be able to get a message from one or other member of my family, but I get nothing and nearly always come away so disheartened. Is there anything coming along to ease this terrible emptiness?"

I had no alternative but to tell Mrs. S. that she was making a mistake. She in fact accepts, as I do, that without doubt there is another life, but, as I told her, life here has to go on as well. I assured her that if she would only find herself a hobby, or join a social club, within six to nine months she would meet a man and this friendship would eventually lead to marriage.

I felt I was doing the right thing in impressing on her that she must be firm with herself and leave spiritualism alone for quite a while, in fairness to those of her family that she had lost. After all, didn't they deserve a rest? If someone in her family wanted to contact her, he would do so in her own home, rather than in a crowded room full of strangers.

I cannot see into my own future, and in many ways I am glad. If I could forecast what life has in store for me as clearly as I can do for others, there would be no surprises left. As it is, I feel that there are quite a few waiting for me around the corner, and there is nothing I like better than to wake up each morning and wonder: What next?

Index

Academy Awards, 185
Anchor, 91, 92
Anger, 92
Animals, 92
Apples, 92
Aquarius, 50, 51, 61, 70-73, 78, 79, 80, 81
Arguments, 92
Aries, 43-46, 53, 67, 76, 79, 80, 81
Armstrong-Jones, Antony, 143
Arnold, Harry, 3, 141, 170, 186, 187
Astrologers, 1-16
Astrology, 17, 38, 40-81, 180-183
Atlas, Dorothy, 151
Attics, 92
Automobiles, 93

Bacharach, Burt, 159
Balconies, 93
Bankhead, Tallulah, 139
Baptism, 93
Barbinel, Maurice, 167
Beauty, 93
Beds, 93, 94
Bibles, 94
Blood, 94
Books, 94

Shape of Things to Come (H. G. Wells), 130
Borley Rectory, 177, 178
Boyd, Stephen, 146
Boyle, Lady, 133
Brain, 18
Branker, Sir Sefton, 15, 16
Bread, 94
Brisson, Carl, 139, 153, 154
Brisson, Frederick, 153
British Film Academy Awards, 8
British Museum, 157
British Red Cross, 142
Brooms, 94
Brushes. *See* Brooms
"Bumps" on head, 19, 20, 21
Burton, Richard, 185

Café de Paris, London, 21, 139, 140, 153
Cakes, 94
Cameron, Arthur, 135, 136
Campbell, Donald, 21, 22, 23
Campbell, Sir Donald, 23
Cancer, 51-53, 64, 75, 77, 80, 81
Candles, 95
Capricorn, 48, 50, 55, 56, 58, 67-70, 78, 80, 81

193

Cards, playing. *See* Cartomancy
Carpets, 95
Carson, Johnny, 185
Cartomancy, 17, 21-34
Cassavetes, John, 7
Cayce, Edgar, 129
Cerebral physiology. *See* Phrenology
Cerise (color), 95
Chains, 95
Chalk, Pauline, 170
Chenhalls, Alfred, 11, 12
Chins, 87, 88
Churchill, Sir Winston, 12, 163, 167
Cigarettes, 95
Clairvoyance, 180-183
Clairvoyants, 1-16
 responsibilities, 123-138
Clocks, 96
Cogen, Alma, 149
Colleano, Bonar, 144
Corbett, Harry H., 6
Coward, Noel, 139
Crystal balls, 17
Curse, making a, 15, 16

Dahl, Arlene, 158
Danger, 96
de Chavigny, Geane Aymes, 129
de Nostradamus, Michel. *See* Nostradamus
Dentists, 96
Devil, 96
Diamonds, 96
Dice, 81-83
Dickinson, Angie, 159
Dietrich, Marlene, 139
Diving, 96
Dixon, Jeane, 130
Douglas, Lewis, 144

Douglas, Sharman, 143, 144
Dowding, Lord Hugh, 166, 167
Doyle, Sir Arthur Conan, 167
Dreams, interpretation, 90-122
 See also individual topics, e.g., Anger, Books, Chains, etc.
Ducks, 96, 97
Dusting, 97

Ears, 88
Earth, 40, 97
Ecstasy, 97
Eggs, 97
Elephants, 97, 98
Emeralds, 98
Entertainment, 98
ESP. *See* Extrasensory perception
Evil, 98
Explosions, 98
Extrasensory perception, 6, 36, 123
Eyes, 11, 17, 83-85, 98, 99, 154

Facial Features, 85-89
 See also Eyes, Mouths, etc.
Falk, Peter, 7
Fame, 99
Fat, 99
Fear, 99
Fire, 99
Fish, 99
Flowers, 99-100
Food, 100
Ford, Glenn, 136
Forehead, 18, 19, 88-89
Freyburg, Larry, 187
Fruit, 100
Future, 17-18

Gains, 100
Gall, Franz Joseph, 18

Gardens, 100
Garland, Judy, 171
Gazzara, Ben, 7
Gemini, 45, 46, 48-51, 61, 62, 72, 76, 77, 79, 80
Gems, 100
Gifts, 100
Gingold, Hermione, 139, 140
Gloom, 100, 101
Graham, Virginia, 127
Grief, 101
Guinness, Sir Alec, 8
Gully, Richard, 135, 136
Guns, 101

Hair, 101
"Halfways," 164
Handkerchiefs, 101
Handwriting, 154
Harris, Richard, 133, 134, 136
Head, 18, 19, 20
Heart, 101, 102
Heath, Edward, 138
Henry VIII, King of England, 157
Hiding, 102
Hills, 102
Hilton, Jack, 35
Hitler, Adolf, 131
Honor, 102
Hopper, Hedda, 145
Horseshoes, 102
Houses, haunted, 169, 170, 171, 177, 178
Howard, Leslie, 12
Hutton, Barbara, 10, 11
Hypnotism, 164, 165

Immortality. *See* Reincarnation
Income, 102

Infants, 103
Injury, 103
Insults, 103
Invalids, 103
Ironing, 104
Itching, 104

Jacobs, David, 141
Jails, 104
Jars, 104
Javits, Jacob, 159
Jeopardy, 104
Jewels, 104
    See also Diamonds, Emeralds, Gems, Zircons
Jilting, 104
Johnson, Lyndon B., 185
Johnston, Richard, 126
Journeys, 105
Jumping, 105
Jupiter, 41

Karma, 164
Kennedy, John F., 147
Kettles, 105
Keys, 105
Kicks, 105
Kings, 105
Kisses, 105, 106
Knees, 106
Knights of the Order of Saint John of Jerusalem, 157
Knives, 106

Ladders, 106
Lang, Dr. Cosmo Gordon, 181
La Rue, Danny, 6, 7
Lateness, 106

Laundering, 106
Leo, 45, 53-56, 70, 77, 79, 80
Lessons, 106, 107
Letters, 107
Libra, 50, 51, 59-62, 67, 72, 73, 77, 78, 80, 81
Loans, 107
Locks, 107
Louis XIV, King of France, 162
Lying, 107
Lyons, Ronald, 134

Magic, 107
Malone, Dorothy, 136
Man, 108
Mann, Roderick, 126
Manners, Dorothy, 185
Map, 108
Marriage, 79-81
Mars, 41
Mayfair Theatre, London, 186
Meat, 108
Medicine, 108
Mercury, 41
Miller, Ann, 136, 137
Mitchum, Robert, 144
Money, 108
Moon, 40
Moore, Roger, 152
Mortimer, Bert, 4
Motion pictures
  Husbands, 7
  I'm All Right, Jack, 8
  The Lady Killers, 8
  A Man for All Seasons, 185
  The Music Man, 37
  My Fair Lady, 37
  Your Past Is Showing, 8
Mouths, 86, 87
Muddles, 108, 109

Munroe, Matt, 138
Music, 109

Nagging, 109
Nahum, Baron, 143, 188
Nakedness, 109
Names, 109
Naylor, Robert, 131, 132
Neck, 109, 110
Neptune, 42
Neville-Willing, Donald, 139
News, 110
Nixon, Richard M., 147, 185
Noises, 110
Norfolk, Duke of, 157
Noses, 85, 86
Nostradamus, 127, 128, 129
Notes, 110
Novak, Kim, 126
Nurses, 110

Oath, 110
Oats, 110-111
Ockendan, Anne, 164, 165
Offers, 111
Oil, 111
Old age, 111
Onassis, Jacqueline Kennedy, 185
"One out," 124
Operas, 111
Oranges, 111
Ox, 111, 112

Pain, 112
Palmistry, 17, 36-37, 39
Paper, 112
Parcels, 112
Parsons, Louella, 145
Pens, 112

Perfume, 112, 113
Personal features, 83-98
Phrenology, 17, 18, 19, 20, 21
Pike, James, 167, 168
Pills, 113
Pisces, 53, 64, 73-75, 79, 81
Pistols, 113
Pixley, Evelyn, 162, 163
Planets, 41-42
Playing cards. *See* Cartomancy
Pluto, 41
Police, 113
Poppy, Sam, 158
Prophecy, 17-89
Psychic flair, 1
Psychic News, 167
Psychics. *See* Clairvoyants

Quarrels, 113
Queen, 113
Questions, 113, 114
Quilts, 114

Rain, 114
Rats, 114
Reconciliation, 114
Reincarnation, 161-179
Religion, 114, 180-183
Revenge, 115
Reventlow, Lance, 10
Rex, Jerry, 2, 3
Ribbons, 115
Rivers, 115
Roses, 115
Rowlands, Gena, 7

Sagittarius, 64-67, 78, 80
Salt, 115
Saturn, 41, 42

Scissors, 115
Scofield, Paul, 185
Scorpio, 53, 58, 62-64, 75, 78, 80, 81
Sellers, Peter, 3, 4, 7, 8, 9, 133
Sex, 75-81
Ships, 115, 116
Shipton, Mother, 129, 130
Shops, 116
Signs, 116
Silk, 116
Silva, Simone, 35, 144, 145
Skull, 18, 19, 20, 21
Smoking, 116
  See also Cigarettes
Spiritualism, 21, 22, 23, 164, 189, 190
Stevens, Stella, 37, 38
Streisand, Barbra, 160
Stringfellow, Olga, 157
Sun, 40
Swaffer, Hannan, 167
Swimming, 116

Taps, 116
Taurus, 46, 47, 48, 58, 59, 76, 79, 80
Taxis, 117
Taylor, Elizabeth, 149, 185
Taylor, Glen, 158
Tea, 117
Teeth, 117
Telepathic willing of evil, 35
Telepathy, 34-36
Television programs
  "Bonanza," 37
  "Girl Talk," 127
  "Maurice Woodruff Predicts," 7, 127, 187
  "Saint," 152
  "77 Sunset Strip," 151
  "Sunday Night at the Palladium," 138

"Tonight Show," 185
Theater
   Come Spy with Me, 7
   Funny Girl, 160
Thomas, Bill, 140, 141, 166, 175, 176, 177
Thought transference. *See* Telepathy
Throat, 117
Tin, 117
Tiredness, 117
Toys, 117-118
Trucks, 118
Tucker, Sophie, 140, 141

Ugliness, 118
Umbrellas, 118
Undressing, 118
Unhappiness, 118
Uniforms, 118, 119
Unkindness, 119
Uranus, 42

Vases, 119
Venus, 41
Versailles Palace, 162, 163
Vexation, 119
Victory, 119
Vinci, Leonardo da, 130
Vines, 119
Violins, 120
Virgo, 48, 56-59, 70, 77, 80, 81
Voices, 120

Wages, 120

Walking, 120
Warner, Ann, 37, 147
Warner, Jack, 37, 147, 155
Warner Brothers, 37
Wars, 120
Webs, 120
Weiss, Robert, 160
Wells, H. G., 130
Whitney, Cornelius Vanderbilt, 159
Whitney, Mrs. Cornelius Vanderbilt, 158, 159
Whittington, Dick, 169
Wigs, 120, 121
Wilson, Harold, 138
Windsor, Duchess of, 10
Windsor, Duke of, 10, 181
Wine, 121
Winston, Helen, 160
Witches, 121
Woodruff, Vera, 9, 10, 15, 36, 130, 140, 141, 142, 153, 163, 168, 176, 178
Worry, 154

Yarn, 21
Yawn, 121
Yellow, 121
Yolk, 121

Zampi, Mario, 8
Zimbalist, Efrem, Jr., 151
Zippers, 121, 122
Zircons, 122
Zodiac, 38, 40-81, 122
Zoos, 122